DEVI BHAGAWATA-PURAN

B.K. Chaturvedi

© Publisher

Publisher	: **Diamond Pocket Books (P) Ltd.**
	X-30, Okhla Industrial Area, Phase-II
	New Delhi-110020
Phone	: 011-40712200
E-mail	: wecare@diamondbooks.in
Website	: www.diamondbooks.in
Edition	: 2025

Devi Bhagwat Purana
By : B.K. Chaturvedi

Introduction

This is the third book of the series of the Puranas undertaken to apprise the youth with our cultural heritage in the language and style they are most familiar with. The Puranas, in fact, dipict the evolution of the ethos in this part of the world and hence they also show the rise and fall of the human values as well in the attempt to set the high norms of living. They reveal to us not only the Dharma as they concieved it but also the ideal routine to live your life usefully and fully. While no attempt has been made to affect any change in the assiduously eulled text, the style has surely been alttered to assimilate the fact not with a blind vision but with an awakened mind. It must, however, be borne in the mind that no alteration in the axiomatic assumptions of the Hinduiam viz. the Karma Theory, the theory of rebirth of the soul till it reaches the level of emancipation and the joint family system, should be assumed. Since the Purana runs along with the help of three set of dialogues, most of the text had been rendered in indirect speech.

Lastly, the auther wants to share his gratitude for **NarendraJi** of **Diamond Publications** whose zeal for making attempt to unearth the gems of our heritage knows no bound. May the tribe multiply as much as to match with the growing population.

—*B. K. Chaturvedi*

"NOR DEEM THE IRREVOCABLE PAST
AS WHOLLY WASTED, WHOLLY VAIN
IF RISING ON ITS WRECKS, AT LAST
TO SOMETHING NOBLER WE ATTAIN"

—*Longfellow from
"The Ladder of St. Augustine"*

Contents

I. Preface

II. The origin of Devi Bhagwat Puran

III. **First Chapter** 19
Haya-greeva's Tale; Madhu-Kaitabh's Story; Urvasi-Puroorava Episode; Birth of Shukadeva; Shukadeva's Quitting His Mortal Coil; Sage Vyas Goes to Hastinapur; The Niyog

IV. **Second Chaprer** 34
Sage Vyas's Birth; Shantanu's Marriages; Bheeshma's Birth; Bheeshma's Terrible Vow; The Pandavas Birth; Parikshita AndJanmejaya

V. **Third Chapter** 45
The Story of The Beginning; Utathya's Enligthtment Sudershana's Worship; The Goddess's Ritual Worship

VI. **Fourth Chapter** 53
The causes of The Krishna Incarnation; Prahled And Nara-Narayana; Sage Bhrigu and Vishnu; The Sage Nara-Narayana's Promise; Lord Krishna's Story

VII. **Fifth chapter** 62
Mahishasur's Slaying; Surath's Story

VIII. **Sixth Chapter** 67
Indra-Vritra's Duel; Nahush's Fall; Vashishtha And Vishwamitra's Confrontation; The Tale of Haihaya Dynasty; Narad-Becomes Monkey-Faced

IX. **Seventh Chapter** 77
Creation Commenced; Sukanya-Chyavan Story; The Ikshavaaku Dynasty; Vashistha And Vishwamitra's Second Feud

X. **Eighth Chapter** 84
Veridicious Harishchandra's Story; Demon Ruru's Tale The Supergods's Arrogance; The Jambudweep And Its Subdivision. The Deseription of Hells; The Ritual Worship of The Super Goddess

XI. **Ninth Chapter** 95
Fight Between Ganga And Saraswati; Radha And Ganga; Tulsi-Shankhchooda's Story; Savitri's Story; Goddess Lakshmi's Origin; Manasa Devi; Mount Vindhya's Anger; Origin of Rudraksha; Counclusion

Preface

The Indian life stream accords great importance to the Puranas not only as the authentic source depicting the religious duty of a person but general conduct in life. Hence the Puranas are part of India's rich heritage. They reveal many stories of human development and depravity in this part of the world and depict the constant endeavour of man to scale now heights after intermittent falls. They, in fact, sum up Indian mind-set-it's transmission from bare rituals to exploring the reason in the knowledge and attaining to metaphysical heights of logic. Subsequently, it is from this height that the ancient sages learnt about supreme bliss attained when the unit merges into the whole; the 'I' surrenders into the supreme conciousness from which issues forth of the stream of selfless devotion called Bhakti.

It is in this process of evolution that the Impersonal form of God and its various attributes-expressions of divinity-gave prefrence to the form of God or the theory of incarnation. The Purana literature centres around the doings of the various incarnation of God. However, this Purana asserts that the Primal Source of all Energy is the Supreme Godess at whose behest the whole universe pulsates. It is this Super Goddess which assigns each God-including the Supre Trinity of Brahma, Vishnu and Mahesh-his function.

Hence She is the entire source of the righteous order of the world, to maintain which She asks his various form to incarnate in accordance to the need felt. Curiously enough the Bhagwata Devi Purana asserts that the Super Goddess manifests herself through five principle forms, giving rise to the comparison of matching this fact with the findings of modern physics. The age old belief of Physics is that energy in the universe is available in five forms only; light, heat, electricity, magnetism and sound. It is also belived that it is electricity which is primal form of energy since capable of manifesting itself in the other forms as well. Compare this analogy with the statement in this Purana and guess upon the possibility that our ancients knew that enregy is available in five forms and its primal form, call it the Super Goddess or Electricity, can also show itself in the rest of the forms. At least at the conception level they were right on the truth that has been verified many eons after their declaring so. It is surely more than a coincidence that they too believed in five forms of energy with one of them is able to manifest in every other form. So in modern parlance it can be said that Super Goddess is the Goddess of Electricity.

However, it is not that the whole edifice of these Purana rests on such scientific truths. Far from it, many are purely legends to highlight one fact. And into the talks and intra-tales many extraneous facts crop in making, at times, it only a book of mythology devoid of any reason. This is because the Indian tradition is not to have a chronological account of history. Here history, in general, continues with a series of narrations. In this Purana also there are as many as three apparent dialogues. As in all other Puranas the 'Sutradhara' (basic narrator) is Seetaji who told all these Purans verbally to the assembly of the sages that gathered in Nemisharanya, a place not far from modern Lucknow. The second pair of interlocutors is Janmejaya, the son of Parikshit and the great grand son of Arjuna of Mahabharat fame, and the great sage Vedavyas, the author or compiler of the grand Mahabharata and many other revered sacred tomes like the Srimad Bhagwata. The third pair is formed by Narada and the sage Narayana of the Nara-Narayan duo. Each pair recounts a story which has been told by one of these pairs. But at times there is enough repetiton. That is why at given places, to avoid the repetition a brief reference has been given with the relevant comment with in parenthesis. It appears that this shortcoming permeates in all the eighteen Puranas, may be, because these stories were included to make one volume a complete work in itself. Neverthless, we have tried to escape this malady by dividing the chapters according to our convience. At times proper sub-tittles have also been given. Yet we have assiduously tried to maintain the flavour of the original.

Although we have given the legends as they have been maintioned in the original yet some of them may appear to be rather 'faith-jerker'. But before forming any decision we request our readership to see as to what is the motive behind such an action. Take for example the legand of Tulsi and Shankhchooda in which Vishnu, the most shrewd God from the Triumvirate, appears as the villain. But once you realise the cause of violating the piety of Tulsi, it becomes clear that his intention is neither selfish nor lecherous. There are scores of such incidents wherein Vishnu appears in this colour for the sake of upholding the righteous order. For that matter, the entire character of Krishna appears fall of seemingly lowly acts but not in the larger interest. In this Purana it has been repeatedly stressed that the Super Goddess often admonishes the three top Gods should they deviate from the righteous path. In fact each Purana differs from its inherent emphasis on concentrating on a particular God. This makes it apparent that they were not created, written or compiled by one person, or a seat or a sect. Although sage Vyas is said to be the author of all the eighteen Purana yet, as has been repeatedly emphasised, the title Vyas was actually a post like we still have the Shankaracharyas. But once a Vyas was chosen, he was given a total free hand to interpret the emphasis in any particular episode or incident.

Nevertheless, the constant emphasis on the superiority of the Mother Goddess in all the Purana is quite striking. Since mother is the origin of all creation she is accorded the highest status in the Hindu pantheism. According to the Samkhya philosophy there are two cosmic entities from the conjunction of which the whole universe is created. One is Purush and the other is Prakriti; while the former is the concept the latter is the manifestation. Although Purush and Prakriti, both are necessary for procreation, status in the context of Prakriti becomes superior as She is seen to beget creation. A mother need not prove her motherhood before her child or the world. But a father has to, and that too, with the help of the mother, who has her credibility above-board. Owing to her procreational capabilities she is considered to be the beacon of all energy. Hence the term 'Shakti' for Mother Goddess which literally means energy. The ancient man, rooted deep in the dogma of the mythlogical lore, could not believe that any human could be as efficient and powerful as to create an exact replica. This led him to believe the presence of the divine element inside a mother. No wonder Gurudeva Rabindranath Tagore wrote: " Since He could not be every where in the world, He created mother!" Hence the raised status of mother in almost all human societies in comparision to any other mortal relation. The concept of motherhood of God, and the Supreme Being manifested in a female form, is bang on the theory of the constant modification of the universe. The cosmos is 'Jagat' (world) and it constantly undergoes changes. The manifested universe is the display of the Shakti or Mahadevi or Supreme Goddess. The infinite sport of the Brahma-shakti (divine power) manitains the equilibrium of the universe. So, one of the most popular epothets of MahaDevi is Jagat-Janani (the Progenitress or Mother of the Universe).

One question may be asked at this juncture as to what is the relevance of these Purana to a modern, computer-age. No matter what age we may be in, our ethos and psyche owe their moulding to the legends that we listen to as the righteous ones. So these Pauranic legends and stories or tales should be read with an open mind while comparing what we believe in and what these assert about. We will rarely find any differance between the two. The Utathya story included in this book highlights the dilemma that we all come across in this modern age. When a hunter asked the sage committed to speaking only truth as to where the deer he had been chasing had gone, what should the sage have done? His telling truth gets that poor animal killed but his not telling it makes him a liar. The moral in the story is that any commitment should not damage the larger interest which ought to be given a higher priority over selfish interest. In fact there are many such stories as go to reaffirm our faith in values Secondly, as far as the sexual overtones of thse stories are concerned we should not miss the fact that in those Primal years when our penel codes were in their infancy, life was a bit less compeatmentalised. It was a free society in the sense that nuptial fidelity was rarely emphasised. Take for example the audacity of Moon (Som) who abducts Vrihaspati's wife in the full knowledge of her husband. Subsequently, when the dispute is resolved by Brahma, the wife is restored to Vrihaspati without his throwing any tantrums. Moreover, in that primal period, may be the fecundity of the females was as much advanced as to make them pregnant even by a mere touch. All such 'Variations from the norms' should be taken with the pinch of self as they could as well the the parts of the interpolatious inserted in the text over the centuries possibly due to foreign influence.

So, what is ahead is the essence-translation of the Purana, with changes only in the style and not in the text, to ease the contents' better comprehension for the modern, computer-oriented generation. And they would find them most logical in thought. The basic thought that emerges from these Puranas including the present one is that a cause must have its affect and hence everyone has to suffer the consequences of one's action no matter who does that action, Gods, men or demons. In fact most of the stories provide the background of the tales that have been popularised by the famous epics like the Mahabharat and the Ramayana. Hence reading them as the 'filler' to the main epics make them additionaly important.'

❑❑

The Origin of Devi Bhagwat Purana

Once the noble souled supreme belivers of God the sages requested Sage Vedavyas's pet disciple Soota Ji: "O Ocean of konwledge! We have felt supreme bliss listening from your blessed mouth the noble doings of Lord Vishnu and Lord Shiv. These historic refererces have enhanced our faith in God and made us wiser than ever before. Now please also tell me as to who is the origin of all power in the universe".

Hearing this, Mahamuni (great Sage) Soota Ji replied: "I am glad you asked this question. Now I tell you about the original or Primal Power of the universe. The details are inscribed in the Holy Devi Bhagwat Purana which is the holiest of the holy books. Now I will tell you not only about how it came to be manifest, but also about the ideal time to read it. I shall also tell as to what wishes of the desirous can be fulfilled by going through this tome devotedly. Also, I will tell you as to who was the blessed person to listen to its narration first and that how its narration should be completed."

The Revelation of the Devi Bhagwat Purana

We all know well that the partial incarnation of Lord Vishnu was Vedavyas, though mortally he is said to be the product of Sage Parashar's union with Satyavati. It was Sage Vedavyas who, in response to the social demands, had divided the entire Vedic knowledge into four parts and made his four main disciples master each part of it. Since that knowledge was not meant for every one, it is for the dull-mitted and deprived humanity that he also wrote eighteen Puranas in which that terse Vedic knowledge had been diluted for its better comprehension by even the lowly most person diluted for its better comprehension by even the lowly most person with various interesting stories, anecdotes and comments thrown in."

Continuing, Soota Ji said: "My Guru, the great Sage Vedavyas entrusted the job of narrating the remaining 17 Purana to noble people but he reserved the 18th Purana, the Devi Bhagwat Purana, whose reading or listening ensures liberation of soul from the cycle of births and deaths, to himself. Eventually he narrated this Purana to Janmejaye (Son of Parikshit and grandson of Abhimanyu of Mahabharat fame). You all know that his father Parikshit had been killed by the serpent Takshak and in order to ensure his father's soul's emancipation, Janmejaya requested the Sage Vedavyas to recite this Purana to him. It was for the first time that by the Divine Goddess's grace that this great Purana dawned upon the sage Vedavyas. When he recited the Holy Purana and the recitation was concluded, the Blessed Goddess appeared before Janmejaya and assured him that the soul of his father had attained to the high state.

The Best Time To Recite This Purana

Soota Ji said: "Listening to this Purana makes the devotees acquire all kinds of spiritual and material prosperity. Even a partial listening to it makes the devotee gain spiritual merit, that merit which a man might get by visiting all the holy places of pilgrimage. Although man attains to high state by various other noble deeds performed in the Satya. Dwapar and Treta Yugas; in Kaliyug this is the only means to emancipate one's distressed soul. It is for the benefit of the people of Kaliyug that the great sage Vyas devised this Holy Purana.

Although its recitation gives beneficial effect no matter when it is done, nevertheless, the ideal time of its recitation is the months of Ashwin, Chaitra, Margsheersha and Ashadha months (roughly corresponding to September, April, December or July months of Gregorian Celender) or during the two Navaratras (one at the on set of summer after the festival of Holi and the other at the onset of winters just before the Dashera festival). It is, in fact, a Yagya that accrues its beneficial effects to the performance that may become his due after performance of a series of noble deeds for centuries together.

Normally the recitation is continued for 9 days non-stop. Even the most wild rogues, thieves, liars, the caluminators of the cow,

Brahmans and the Gods or Gurus get reformed by listening or reading this Purana. The text claims that

"Tatha na Ganga na Gaya na Kashi na Navmish,
na Mathura na Pushkaram!
Punati sadyah Badrivanam na Yatha
hi Devimaph esha Viprah"

[The religious merit that accures to one by visiting all the holy pilgrim places like bank of the Ganga river; the holy cities like Kashi, Mathura or Gaya or the sacred spot like Naimisharanya, becomes due to the performer of the Yagya of reciting this Holy Devi Bhagwat Purana]

According to the Soota Ji on the 8th day of the lunar bright fortnight of Ashwini, the Goddess's idol should be placed upon the golden throne and after due consecration the holy Katha of the Blessed Devi should be recited by a noble and learned Brahmana. So high is the religious merit that the person who does this Yagya recieves that; even if he chants just one Shloka everyday he ensures the Blessed Devi's shedding Her grace upon him.

The Great Potency of This Blessed Purana

The places where this holy Purana is recited get rid of all the natural calamities like drought, floods, earth-quakes and the affliction due to presence of the evil spirit etc. The reciter and the listner of this Purana are spared of all the physical, mental and financial troubles. Alluding to an ancient tale to highlight this Purana's great potency to set aside all problems, Soota Ji said: "It was owing to Vasudeva's (Lord Krishna's father) listening to this great Purana that Krishna returned home safely after defeating Jambavant and retrieving the lost Syamantaka Gem. This Purana's recitation had ensured Krishna's safe arrival since as soon as the recitation of this Purana concluded, there appeared Krishna with the gem and a bride for himself to the great delight of his father."

The Syamantak Gem's Tale

Hearing the reference of this incident, on the sages 'insistence Soota Ji recited this story in details.'

There was a man in Dwarika called Satrajit. He was an ardent worshipper of Lord Sun. Propitiated by his worship the Lord appeared before him and granted a wonder-gem radiant with such a dazzling light that the people of Dwarika thought as though Lord Surya (the Sun) had given Satrajit his own radiance. That wonder-gem used to give about '8 bhara' (nearly 80 tolas) gold everyday. Lord Krishna thought this gem should have been given to the royal treasury of Dwarika to help the state ameliorate the suffering of the needy people more conveniently and hence he asked Satrajit to give it to the royal coffers. But Satrajit refused. Later, Satrajit's brother Prasenjit took this wonder gem along when he went for hunting. Consequently, the gem was found missing. Whereupon Satrajit suspected Krishna to have stolen it since the latter had eyed it greedily. He openly blamed Lord Krishna for stealing the gem. In order to prove his innocence Lord Krishna went in search of that wonder gem, taking a clue from Prasen's friends about the path he might have taken. Meanwhile, a lion had devoured Prasen and the gem and happened to reach near a cave where the fabled bear, Jamavanta, (of Ramayana fame) was residing. The bear happened to kill that lion and took along the gem with him having extracted it from the lion's stomach. Reaching his cave he gave that gem to his daughter called Jambavati.

In the meantime, searching for the gem Lord Krishna also reached near Jambavanta's cave. There, when he espied a young female bear playing with that gem, he recognised it. But Jambavanta, hearing the commotion, came out of his cave and challanged Krishna for a duel. While fighting the duel Jambvant realised that he was fighting against his chosen Lord Ram in a different form. He apologised to Krishna and not only returned the gem but also gave his daughter in marriage to Lord Krishna. When the gem was brought back to Dwarika, Vasudeva, who, all this while, was listening to the recitation of the Devi Bhagwat Purana, was delighted. He had started the Devi-Bhagwat Yagya on the advice of his Guru Garga who told him: "Listen to this great Purana to get rid of any problem." His words proved right. As the recitation ended his beloved son Krishna returned trimphantly with the gem and yet another bride for himself.

Agastya-Skand Dialogue

Soota Ji, then, narrated another episode to highlight the great efficacy of this Purana.

Once Skanda (also called Kartikeya) was listening to ancient noble tales from the great Sage Agastya. While the Sage told about the efficacy of a variety of deeds to provide one solace, comforts and prosperity, but that Lord Shiv's son, Skanda, was not amused. He requested the sage to tell about the ultimate source of all universal energy whose glories might give him full satisfaction. Whereupon Sage Agastya narrated the following story to impress upon Skanda the power of this Devi Bhagwat Purana.

Sudymna Regains His lost Manhood

Vivaswavasn's son Shraddha Deva had no issue. In order to get a son he performed a Yagya on the advice from sage Vashishtha. But while pronouncing the Mantra during the Yagya he happened to utter 'Putree deeyatam' instead of the intended 'Putra deeyatam'. With the result, Shraddha Deva got a daughter named 'Ila'. The king Shraddha Deva was unhappy. He rushed to the great sage Vashishtha and confessed about his mispronouncing the Mantra which made him get a daughter and not a son as he longed for. He further requested: "O Sage! Could it be possible now that may daughter Ila may again become a male." Thawing with mercy the sage, used his Yogic power to convert that daughter into a son who then came to be known as Sudyumna.

When Sudyumna grew into a robust young man he went for hunting. But, passing from one Jungle to the other, he happened to lose his way and reached the prohibitive area which was reserved for Lord Shiv and Parvati's enjoying their amorous plays. Parvati had ruled that if any male member happened to enter that reserved Jungle, he is sure to become a female. Consequently, as Sudyumna reached there he became a girl again. Not only he but all his companions, even the horses etc, also became female.

Once while wandering as a girl, Sudyumna happened to reach before the saint Budha's hermitage. The Sage was won over by the girl's charms and they united physically to beget a son named Puroorava. Having stayed for many years in that hermitage, Sudyumna was now longing to get back to his previous life as man. So he went back again to his family priest Vashishtha. Realising the agony his 'Yajaman' was going through Vashishtha prayed Lord Shiv. Duly propitiated, Lord Shiv told Vashishtha that henceforth Sudyumna would stay one month as female and one month as male. But since this hardly satisfied Vashishtha or Sudyumna, the sage again worshipped Bhagwati Devi Jagdamba who advised Vashishtha to go to Sudyumna's house and start worshipping her (the Goddess) afresh. She also advised to start her 'Navanha Parayana' [non-stop worship for 9 days].

Going back home with the sage, Sudyumna waited till 8th day of the lunar bright half of the month of Ashwini, then started the ritual worship of the great Goddess. The Devi was duly propitiated and Sudyumna again became a full fledged man. Then Vashishtha made him sit on the royal throne.

How To Listen To This Holy Purana

While narrating this incident of Sudymna's regaining his male form with the help of sage Vashishtha, Soota Ji advised the entire assembly of the holymen that like the auspicious time is divised by the astrologers for a girl's marriage, so should also be done before starting the formal recitation of this holy Purana. Althogh any time would be auspicious but the best time is in nine days of the Navaratra period. Invitation should be formally sent to all friends, relations, acquaitances, holy brahmanas, respectable Kshatriyas, even their women folk. Even the pious Shoodras shouid also be invited for the function. There is no compulsion that every one shoud attend the full session. Even partial attedance in this recitation can also bring very good results.

Then the venue should be sanctified by spreading evenly the little of cow-dung-paste. Then the pedestal should be placed on that spot which may be covered by a canopy. On the pedestal should be placed the icons or idols of the Goddess with her flag fluttering above the canopy.

Then, a learned and pious Brahmana having good prounciation and loud voice should be chosen for reciting the Purana. After the ritual clearing activities all the curious devotees should assemble at the venue and the realation should start after the day break. Before starting and ending the part of the recitation, the Goddess must be invoked through her orisons and Aaratis. During the period this 'Katha' (recitation of the Goddes's doings) lasts, all should sleep on the floor, have frugal diet while keeping mind least occcupied in mundane affairs Alcohol, drugs, narcotic herbs and all extremely spicy food containing onion, garlic etc. should be forgiven totally during this period.

When the recitation is over, it should be concluded with devotional songs sung in the praise of the Goddess. Then the host must offer the due fees, cloth and other auspicious material to the priest with some suitable gifts to all those who came to his house to listen to the Grand Purana. Then the priest should be fed on choicest food items in the company of the unmarried young girls who are deemed to be the representatives of the Goddess herself.

Concluding the narration centring on this Purana's glories, Soota Ji said: "This is the best Purana among all the 18 Purana. Like Ganga among the rivers, Shankar among the deities, the Ramayana among the epics, the Sun among the sources of light, Earth among those known for patience, Ocean among those known for their depth and Gayatri among the Mantra, so is this Devi Bhagwat Purana among all the Puranas; the magic wand to ward off all mindane troubles."

❐❐

First Chapter.......

When all the Sages assembled there including Shaunak requested Sage Vedavyas's pet disciple Soota Ji to recite them the Devi Bhagwat Purana, Soota Ji said: "This Purana contains twelve Chapters, three hundred eighteen sub chapters and eighteen thousand Shlokas Although it contains the details about different Manus and their descendants etc., yet since it delineates all the three. Sattviki, Rajasi and Tamasi (noble, royal and dull) forms of the inherent energy in the whole universe which are represented by Saraswati, Mahalakshmi and Mahakali through their attributes, this Purana gathers special merit and significance and hence it outscores others in effectiveness."

"It may be recalled that in every Dwapar Age of the every cycle, there dawns a Vyas who edits all the holy scriptures and compiles their gist in the Mahabharat. This Purana was first recited by Vyas Ji to his son Shukhdeva who was not brought into the world through any vagina. While the father was reciting this Purana to his son, being the pet disciple of the Sage Vyas, Soota Ji, also happened to listen this soul liberating Purana. While highlighting its noble impact Soota Ji said that: "I can even guarantee that those who listen to it go to heaven for sure."

When the other saints insisted on knowing more about the birth legend of Shukhdeva, Soota Ji said: "Once Vyas Ji was passing through the jungles on the bank of the river Saraswati. He espied there a couple lovingly caressing their new-born child. This scene made his heart long for having a son of his own. He thought that a sonless father will neither have his lineage assured nor he would get oblation to quench his soul's thrust after death. Moreover, who would be there to provide him any support in the old age? Manu, Yagyavalkya and other great seers concur that birth of a son assures liberation and makes the father carve a niche for himself in the heaven." Feeling great agony due to this shortcoming in his life, Vyas Ji decided to hold a Yagya with the intention of geting a son. While he was thinking as to which deity to be worshipped to have his this longing fulfilled-Indra, Sun, Varuna, Vishnu, Ganesh or Skanda-he found the divine sage Narada close to him. Vyas Ji duly honoured Narada and placed his quandary before him. Then Narada told him about one incident." Once Brahma found even Lord Vishnu indulging in difficult penance. He asked: "O Blessed Lord, you are the sustainer of this entire universe. In my form you create while in Shankar's form you destroy the creation. Since you are omnipotent, who are you worshipping then?" Vishnu replied: "Although every one in the universe thinks that the final authority in this universe rests in we three, yet the fact is that we three too, are only the instrument to convey the dictates of that Supreme Power, the Primal Source of all energy."

Vishnu further said: "Brahma! you are wise enough to know that I am also dependent upon that very Primal Energy the Great Goddess. Whenever I get weak She comes to my rescue. You know that once I fought against the demonus Madhu and Kaitabh for about a thousand years but had failed to score victory over them. Then it was only that Primal Energy-the Devi-who provided me strength to eventually slay those demons. So," concluding his advice, Narad said: "I think, sage Vyas, that you should try to propitiate that ultimate energy, the blessed Devi."

Continuing his narration, Soota Ji said: "Once Lord Vishnu had to fight against demons non-stop for about ten thousand years. Getting extremely tired, Vishnu found a picturesque spot where be started relaxing. And all of a sudden he was fast asleep due to that extra toil.

Haya-Greeval's Tale

"Meanwhile, all Gods led by Brahma reached Vishnu's abode Vaikuntha, to invite Vishnu for a massive Yagya performance. When they found Vishnu missing from Vaikuntha, they asked their Guru,

Vrihaspati, to find as to where the Blessed Lord might be. Vrihaspati, through his Yogic powers found the spot where Vishnu lay sleeping. All the Gods immediately went to that spot but since Vishnu was in a deep slumber, they failed to wake him up.

"But since on that Yagya had depended the Gods security, it was necessary to wake the Lord up. Sensing the God's worry Brahma created termite (white ants) and ordered it to nibble at Vishn's taut bow-string. The creator thought this world create much noise, enough to wake Vishnu up, since the tant bow-string was sure to snap with a great bang.

But as the termite ate away a part of the tant bow-string, the bow straighted with such a force that the upward thrust of the end of the bow hacked Vishnu's head away, which fell in the Lavana Sagar (Salty Sea).. Seeing Vishnu headless the Gods began to weep uncontrollably.

Seeing the Gods' plight, the creator consoled them, "Be composed, Gods! It was our sheer bad luck. This appeared to have happed as willed by that Supreme Goddess with whose command Shiv had once beheaded me while his organ had also fallen away. And it was she only who restored our missing limbs. She is, infact, our only hope. Only she can restore Vishnu's head."

Getting this hint from Brahma the Gods began to hymn the glories of that Supreme Goddess, who appeared when duly propitiated and said: "Worry not, divinities! It was my will which made Vishnu lose his head. I'll tell you as to why I willed so. Once seeing the visage of Lakshmi Vishnu had guffawed in contempt. Lakshmi was quite upset. She felt that Vishnu did so only because of his waning love for her and enhancing love for the other co-wife. Hence she cursed Vishnu that one day he would be head-less." Continuing her narration, the Great Goddess said: "In fact this has been done with a special purpose. The demon Hayagreeva (One with the head of a horse) had become very powerful owing to his receiving a boon from me. Though he wanted the boon of immortality yet those are born in this world must die. So I gave him the boon with the condition that any one with a horse's head planted instead of his own head would be able to kill Hayagneerva. Now plant a horse's head on Vishnu's trunk and let him fight with that

Hayagreeva in this form. After this Vishnu would get back his head."

As advised by the Great Goddess, the Gods did so. As soon as Vishnu got the horse's head he challanged that deadly demon Hayagreeva and slayed him in no time. The Gods were delighted to have Vishnu soon endowed with his normal head.

Madhu-Kaitabh's Story:

Narrating yet another episode to highlight the Goddess's immense power, Narada told Vyas: "O Son of Satyawati! Many eons ago when once Lord Vishnu was resting on his serpent coil-bed in the ocean of milk, out emerged from his ears the fifth in the form of two deadly demon. Madhu and kaitabh. As soon as they were created they assumed deadly form and became very powerful. At this very time guided by a divine voice they went to perform a vigorous penance to learn the very purpose of their creation. They concentrated their devotion on to the Great Goddess and worshipped her so devotedly that she eventually appeared before them and granted them the boon that they wanted.

With that boon the demons became invincible. They unleashed a reign of terror all over the creation. They had the temenity of even challanging the Creator, Brahma. They yelled: "Get away from your this lotus seat which is meant only for the brave and not for the coward. So either you fight with us or get away from your exalted seat".

Brahma was hardly prepared for this challange. He sought shelter under Lord Vishnu's grace. But Vishnu was lost in his Yoga sleep. When all attempts to wake up Vishnus failed Brahma deduced: "It appears it is Vishnu who's under sleep's control and not vice-versa. So unless I seek help from that Goddess who controls the Yoga-Nidra (Yoga-sleep), I won't be able to rouse Vishnu from his slumber."

"Then Brahma began to hymn the great Goddess glories : "O Goddess, the Primal energy controlling all universe! Your sportive acts are not decipherable. Now I seek your shelter. Please destroy these demons or make Vishnu shed his Yoga sleep to rescue me from these dreadful existences."

Hearing Brahma's prayers the Goddess in no time made Vishnu come awake. Brahma was delighted at recieving such an early answer to his prayers."

While narrating these incidents Narad advised Vedavyas that he should make his prayers direct to the Supreme Goddess. He further said: "So, O sage, as soon as Vishnu was awake he asked Brahma the cause of his distress. Hearing about Madhu and Kaitabh causing great fear in Brahma's mind, Vishnu accompanied him to go to the demons.

Seeing Brahma again peacefully settled in his lotus seat, the demous challanged him for a duel which Vishnu accepted on Brahma's behalf. Then they confronted Vishnu. Their fight continued for five thousand years with none of them winning. While the demons fought one by one, Vishnu was feeling quite tired. According to the rules of the duel, Vishnu asked them a period of respite to which the demons agreed.

During that period of rest Vishnu thought over the reason which made the demons so powerful. He soon learnt that the supreme Goddess's boon had made them invincible. Then Vishnu also sought succour from the Goddess. Getting propitiated, the Goddess assured Vishnu of lending him a helping hand in his fight against the demons. As the fight ensued again, Vishnu begged help from the Goddess. And lo and behold: There appeared a comely damsel in the arena. The demons were so enchanted of that damsel's beauty that they suspended the fight and began to look at that beautiful lady wistfully. The love-bug had bitten them and dispite Vishnu's challange they kept on admiring the lady's beauty. Then Vishnu said: "O kay! If you are not willing to fight and you want peace, you may have your boons from me."

The haughty demons thundred: "We are not beggars of any body's favour. On the contrary, if you desire you may have any boon from us."

Vishnu thought of utilising this golden opportunity He said: "Then tell me: how can you two be slain?"

Hearing this question the demons were perterbed for a moment. But in order to keep their promise true, they said: "We can be slain only if we are struck in a waterless region.

While this fight was on in water, Lord Vishnu, getting this hint, immidiately lifted the entire water surface by raising his knees. With the result, the plain the demons were on thus far became water-less. As Vishnu was about to strike them, the demons magnified their body-size by their demoniac power as much as to make them again touch water with their bodies. Seeing this the Lord of Lakshmi made his knees as big as to again bring them out of water. As they were out of water, Vishnu didn't delay for a second and struck his charged Sudardhan Chakra at their bodies which hacked off the demons heads in a trice."

Hearing this episode which made Vyas Ji realise the Supreme power of the Goddess, he left for the Sumeru Mount to pray the Goddess to provide him with a son to continue his lineage. He remained in penance for a long time. His body grew very weak and his hair turned almost grey. At last his prayers were answered after as many as 100 years' worship. The Supreme Goddess with Adi Shiv appeared before Vyas to grant him a popular and extremely learned son.

Vyas returned to his hermitage getting the desired boon. When he reached there he thought of performing a Yagya. To produce fire he took two dry twings of the rice plant and rubbed them against each other. However while busy in performing the Yagya he thought as to how would he be able to get a son in the absence of a wife. Now, while he was thinking of procuring a good wife for him, he spotted the divine dauseuse (Apsara) passing by in her aerial route. Although he was charmed by that divine dauseuse, —"In case I copulate with her, won't I be meeting the same fate as Puroorva met bound in the love of another dausense Urvashi? Lest people may laugh at my uncontrollable sexual lust as well?"

Urvasi Pooroorva Episode

When this episode was referred to in the narration of Soota Ji, the listening noble saints were curious about knowing this episode of Puroorva and Urvashi as well.

Soot Ji said: "The story starts this way. Once the wife of the divine mentor Vrihaspati, Tara, went to meet her friend, the wife of the Moon God. But seeing Tara's beauty Somadeva (the Moon God) grew so enamoured of her that he didn't let Tara return. Tara was also drawn to him. For many years they stayed together. When Vrihaspati, who was absent, returned and learnt about his wife's absence and the Moon-God's this evil deed, he rebuked the latter and reprimanded his wife, Tara, to return home. But detecting a streak of love lurking in Tara's heart for himself Somadeva offered a counter-rebuke to Vrihaspati, saying: "I never went to invite her. Your wife herself came to me. When you can't bind your wife with your love, you have no right to rebuke others for her infidelity. Now she is my beloved and I can't return her to you against her wish, no matter what you say."

Diappointed at recieving such a contumelious treatment from Somedeva, Vrihaspati returned empty-handed. Although Vrihaspti made yet another attempt to bring his wife back, yet this time the Moon-Goods' sentiments didn't allow him any access to the palace and threw the divine Guru out unceremoniously. This made Vrihaspati start imprecating Some-Deva out side the latter's palace. Enraged, when Vrihaspati threatened Some-Deva with a deadly curse, the latter come out of the palace and said: "I care two hoots for a lecher like you are. Even otherwise a beauty like Tara would be misplaced in a beggar's house like you appear. Nevertheless, if you are feeling the uncontrolable sexual charge, I can offer you any maid from my palace who shall help in releasing your pant-up charge. But I shall not part with Tara no matter what you do!"

Bearing such contemptuous attitude shown by Moon, Vrihaspati sought solace in the divine-king Indra's shelter who tried to pacify Vrihaspati with the assurance that he would soon take the Moon-God to task for this offence. But when Indra summoned Moon to explain his behaviour, the latter gave him the rebuff, saying that persons like him (Indra) who never minded enjoying other's women had just no right to demand explanations from others. This rebuff almost compelled Indra to wage a war against the arrogant Moon.

Meanwhile, the demon-Guru Shukracharya advised Moon to keep sticking to his guns, and promised all help through the Mantra and Tantra shakti in his feud against the divine Guru. owing to Shukracharya's influence even Lord Shiv sided with Moon.

Consequently, Indra attacked Moon and a fierce bettle ensured between them. Setting this deadly war among the Gods over a woman, Brahma intervened and asked Moon to return Tara to Vrihaspati. He also warned Moon: "Should you defy my orders I would make Vishnu cause your destruction". Shukracharya, who had all though been the supporter of Moon criticised the creator for being so partial in setting the feud. Brahma then also asked Shukracharya to behave. Eventually Shukracharya advised Moon to obey the Creator's command as his welfare lied in it only.

Vrihaspati returned home with his wife Tara in toe. At due time Tara gave birth to a boy. Deeming him to be his own son, Vrihaspati got all the rituals ceremoniously completed. But when the Moon learned about the birth of this boy, he laid his claim upon him, claming that he was born of his seed. Hence he demanded posession of the boy from Vrihaspati who blankly refused to accept it. Again the feud gathered momentum. Seeing the tempers on the both sides running high, Brahma again intervened and asked Tara to truthfully name the real sire of the boy. Bowing her head in shame Tara said: "The truth is that this boy is born of Moon's seed.". Whereupon, Brahma gave that boy to Moon. Moon called him Budh (Mercury) and lovingly reared him.

Continuing the narration, Soota Ji said: "Once unclad Parvati was sitting on Lord Shiv's lap and both were engaged in amorous dalliance. Suddenly in that very garden happened to reach Shukra and other sage for the Lord of the Universe's (Shiv) Darshan. But they felt quite abashed and mortofied seeing the prohibitive scene. In order to escape from that embrrasment they quickly went ahead bowing their heads to the Lord. But Parvati felt very much ashamed. Seeing his spouse so hurt, Lord Shankar declared that area around his abode to be inaccessible for any male and also announced that any male transgressing in to that area would instantly become female. It was king Sudyumna's bad luck that he unknowingly entered the prohibitive region and became Ila. (The story has been explained before). From the union of Ila and Budh was born Puroorva.

When Puroorva became young he acquired a kingdom. It was around that time that the divine danseuse Urvashi had come to pass some time on the earth due to a curse of a sage. Puroorva happened to see her and he was so entranced by her beauty that he proposed to marry Urvashi. But Urvashi put forth her three condition for marriage.
1. That Puroorva would always feed her on food made from Ghee.
2. That apart from during copulation with her, Puroorva would never appear unclad before her.
3. That the King would tend two pet lambs of Urvashi with loving care ensuring full security and safety to them.

Possessed by Urvashi's charms, Puroorva readily accepted the conditions. Then Urvashi also warned him that should he ever break any of the conditions, she would be free to leave him without any advance notice and would straight away return to heaven. Puroorva also accepted this warning and began to dwell happily with Urvashi.

Meanwhile, Indra found heaven rather deserted in the absence of Urvashi. He asked his two gandharva assistants to do something to make Urvashi return to heaven. Both of them quitely reached earth and seizing their opportunity when Urvashi and Puroorva were busy copulating and managed to steal the danseuse's two pet lambs. While they did so, the lambs cried and their crying was heard by Urvashi. She immediately asked Puroorva to go and save the lambs as per his promise. Since Puroorva was naked at that time, he hesitated a bit to go after the lambs unclad. But Urvashi thought that he was hesitating out of his cowardice. She started calling him timid and pusillanimous. "Oh God! What a coward is my husband!" At last, Puroorva was forced to chase the thieves of the lambs in his unclad state. As he approached close to the cunning Gandharvas, they lighted a lamp before Puroorva. With the result, Urvashi, who came after the king, saw the king naked in that light. Since they were not copulating, Poorva had, thus, broken the second condition. This made Urvashi leave the king for ever and return to heaven.

When the king returned he was impatient seeing the dauseuse missing. Severely torn in the seperation from his beloved, the king began to cry uncontrollably. Then forgetting about his state duties and administration he began to roam about everywhere in the search of Urvashi. Fortunately, one day he spotted her in Kurukshetra, and requested her to accompany him again. But giving him a piece of a bitter advice that ' those man who are infatuated by women are called fools,' she went away, The King was still madly chasing her. But she disappeared making a fool of that king.

Continuing the narration, Soota Ji said: "Although the fate of Puroorva detracted sage Vyas from seeking physical union with that dausense Ghritachi, neverthless, he had grown so much sexually overcharged that he ejaculated, making his seed fall into a leaf-cup. It was at due time that from that very leaf-cup Shukadeva was born. That is why Shukadeva is often referred to as born from a leaf-cup.

Birth of Shukadeva

Vyas Ji reared his son Shukadeva performing all the necessary ceremonies. As his son became grown up, in order to continue his lineage he requested him to marry. But Shukadeva refused the suggestion point blank. Then Vyas Ji told his son: "Dear Son! All the severe penances that I had performed will go waste if you don't marry. If you fail to continue my lineage, what is the purpose that you are born for?" But this plea failed to influence the determined Shukdeva. He thought marriage, wealth, progency as the source of all kinds of troubles. Hence he considered married life to be most unwanted option. Even then citing the examples of Lord Shiv and other Gods Vyas still insisted that his son should marry.

Now Shukdeva was quite surprised. He deemed his father to have been well versed in all scriptures and knowledge who also knew that marriage had hardly added to the happiness of any God, let alone the mortals. But Vyas Ji again said: "The basic duty of a father is to make his son tread the correct path" Then Shukhdeva couldn't keep quite" "Father! you know well that all these mortal relations are transistory and impermanent. More important than continuing the lineage is devoting this rarely recieved human birth, that too in a brahman's family, to realising the ultimate goal : proximity with the Ultimate." Then Shukdeva told Vyas about his final decision of becoming a Sanyasi (ascetic), adding "If you are really my well wisher, then instruct me in the Ultimate Knowledge of Self and self-realisation."

"Son! If you are so determined and your mind is so mature even in the prime of youth, perhaps you are the most deserving person to listen to the essence of all scriptural and spiritual knowledge, the Devi Bhagwat Purana. Listen it with full concentration as it enriches your knowklegdge, sharpens your intelligence and makes your discretion quite mature. Now listen it attentively."

Then Vyas Ji started narrating this Purana to his son. Once, when the whole earth was under water of deluge and Lord Vishnu, like a child, was lying on a leaf-kept on a tree, he started thinking : "Who made me reach this stage? Who was it that made me omnipotent and omniscient!" Then he suddenly heard the clandestine voice of the Supreme Goddess: "I it was who made you reach this stage"

Vishnu was still bewildered: "How come this Banyan grew at this place when the whole world is under water? And most surprisingly how I am reduced to being only an infant lying atop it on a long leaf. And what I am supposed to do when I confront the Supreme Goddess who claims to have wrought the entire situation?

Reminding Vishnu of his past the Goddess said "Due to the effect of the illusion cast by me you have forgotten me. Else you know that it is my power that manifests in the Sattavie, Rajesik and Tamasik forms all over the Universe. It is only that power that makes the lotus shoot out of Vishnu's navel with Brahma seated on it with enough powers to set the process of creation rolling. Subsequently, Shiv gets manifest from the brow region of Brahma. Each of them has one basic attribute marking their action. While Brahma shows the Sattavik, Vishnu Rajasik and Shiv Tamasik attributes of my power". This whole idea was expressed by the Supreme Goddess in half a Shloka which conveys the essence of the Devi Bhagwat Purana.]

After sometime Brahma emerged from the lotus shooting out of the navel of Vishnu and when he asked Vishnu as to whom be, the Super Lord, was worshipping, Vishnu said: "The one and only one who causes yours, mine and the whole Universe's existence. I am chanting that half a shloka: "SHARANYE TRIYAMBIKE GAURI

NARAYANI NAMOSTUTE' to concentrate my mind on the Spreme Goddess's visage."

Continuing the narration Vyas Ji said to his son, Shukadeva: "It was on Brahma's request that Vishnu revealed this secret to Brahma who, in turn, out of paternal affection disclosed it to Narad. It was sage Narad who shed his grace upon me by revealing it to me. Now this secret revealing of the Supreme Goddess glory, which gives to the learner all material and spiritual wealth and fame, is being given to you. Now listen it attentively."

Shukadeva's Quitting His Mortal Coil

Having told this Soota Ji further said: "But as Shukadeva learnt this great Purana from his father, Vyas Ji, he grew all the more averse to wordly bonds and leaving home he setlled in Kailash to perform vigorous penance. Eventually going into his Yoga-trance he quitted his mortal coil.

Sage Vyas Goes To Hastinapur

"Getting this saddening news Vyas Ji was quietly perturbed. He immediately bade adieu to his well-wishers, relations and pet disciples like Vaishampayan, Jaimini, Sumant and left to his birth place on the bank of river Ganga to seek solace in his mother Satyavati's lap. In fact Vyas Ji had given his word to Satyavati that whenever she would call him, he would come to her. He was listening to that secret call from Satyavati. As he reached his maternal grandfather Nishad's place, Nishad welcomed him and told him that having married king Shantanu, Satyavati was now in Hastinapur. After Shantanu's death his son, Chitrangeda, was installed as the king but he was killed by drunken Gandharva. Then his younger brother, Vichitraveerya was made the king of Hastinapur. Since he was not physically robust, it was difficult to get a suitable bride for her. Ultimately, Bheeshma, the eldest son of Shantanu, who had refused to be a king due to his severe vow of neither marrying nor ever ascending to the throne which earned him the title Bheeshma (his real name was Devavrata), decided to forcibly make Kashi King's three daughters: Amba, Ambika and Ambalika, marry Vichitraveerya. But out of these three girls, one Ambalika refused to marry him and she went back to her beloved the king Shalva. Though Vichitraveerya had two wives, he failed to produce any son from them. Eventually after ruling for 9 years he too expired, leaving the throne of Hastinapur heirless. Although bound by his vow, Bheeshma never accepted kingship yet with Satyavati he acted as the care-taker-ruler of the Kingdom of Hastinapur. But Satyavati was worried for heir-less kingdom was bound to be userped by other kings. Since Bheeshma had refused to marry, there was no chance of Hastinapur getting a king. Seeing the dynasty getting its lineage stopped, Satyavati decided to call her son 'Vyas' whom she had begotted prior to her marriage to Shantanu. At last she decided to make Vyas give his seed to Vichitraveerya's wife. This was what Bheeshma had also adviced: "Mother! Get a good brahman from a noble family to have the Niyoga (marriage for the limited period only for getting a son) consummated." Satyavati thought Vyas to be the best choice. That was why she had mentally summoned Vyas.

The Niyog

As Vyas reached the palace of Hastinapur, having learnt all these details from Nishaad, he met Bheeshma first. He took Vyas to Satyavati who ordered Vyas to establish Niyoga marriage with her daughter-in-law. He produced Dhritarashtra from his union with Ambika. But that son, Dhritarashtra, was born blind, So Vyas had to have physical union with Amba as well. But this time the physical union produced, Pandua son with a chronic disease. Vyas who also had physical union with a maid of the palace who produced Vidur. Ultimately a unanimous decision of the family made Pandu the king as Dhritarashtra was not fit to be a king due to his being blind and Vidur couldn't have been made the king because he was the son of a mere maid. This way having assured the continuity of the dynasty under Satyavati's order, Vyas Ji returned to his hermitage. The irony of Vyas's life had been that having lost his own son, Shukadeva, he was asked to produce several sons but none of whom could he claim to be his own. But there in lies his greatness that having suffered a great agony he sacrificed his personal happiness for the sake of continuing the line of the dynasty his mother had been married unto at the behest of his mother.

❏❏

Second Chapter.......

When the sages heard about Satyavati, the mother of Chitrangada and Vichitraveerya being also the mother of Vyas (Vyas Dweipayan as he was born on a dweep or island), they were curious about getting full details. Sensings these nobles curiosity Soota Ji obliged them by telling about the episode. This was what he told.

Sage Vyas's Birth

Long ago there dwelled a king in Chedi Pradesh, named Upanichara who was of very religious temperament, ascetic by nature and great believer in the superiority of the Brahmana. He had a beautiful wife named Ginika who was extremely beautiful. She bore five brilliant sons for a king. Once the king had gone for hunting and in jungle he missed his wife so much that he ejeculated. In order to save his seed he collected it in a leaf-cup and orderd his pet fallen to go and have it diposited in his wife's vagina. This way, he sent the message to his wife, she would concieve. But as the falcon was taking it, another big bird thought it to have been some edible. So it swiped at the cup, making the seed fall in the river.

It was exactly at that moment a divine danseuse called Admika, while swimming in that river felt greatly sexually charged. She spotted a brahman lost in meditation on the bank of the river. She asked him to have sexual union with her. But when the determined brahman didn't respond to her overtures, she came as much close to him as to caress his body. This made the brahman blow up in rage and he cursed the danseuse to become a fish. But on repeated requests, he modified his curse: "You shall be released from that form and regain your original form when you are able to produce human being from your womb."

Meanwhile, the seed of the king had fallen into the river. This fish (the danseuse) drank it and she concieved as well. After ten months, that fish was netted by a fisher-man. He was surprised to see so fat a fish. In greed he tore apart the fish's stomach and out emerged from it two human figures; One of them being a boy and other a girl. While the boy was entrusted to the king's (state's) custody, the girl was given to the fisher-man. When she grew up, this girl, having a typical fish like smell ever emanating from her body, began to help her adopted father in his work whose main occupation was to row the boat across the river and help the people cross the river on payment. Dwelling on the bank of the river Yamuna the father and the daughter earned their wherewithal this way.

Once the great sage Parashar happened to reach there in the process of his visiting all the holy spots. When he reached the bank of that river Yamuna, the boat-man, Nishad, was having his food. Seeing a noble sage desiring to go across the river, he asked her daughter to take him across in the boat. While sitting in the boat the sage was captivated by that girl's beauty. He immidiately desired physical union with that girl. But she deterred him, reminding him of his high family and status visavis her own. But the sage was so much sexually charged that he immidiately took the girl on to his lap. When the girl said that she stank like a fish, using his Yogic powers the sage made her body emanate a pleasant smell. Then the girl objected to copulating in the day time with many people looking on, and requested the sage to wait till the darkness enveloped them, The sage cast such illusion that they appeared covered by a thick fog, thus becoming invisible to others. At last the girl said: "O Sage, enjoying my youthful body you will go away. What will I do if I concieve with your seed in me? Can I face my society? Won't the people cast aspersion on an unmarried girl getting pregnant? What, then, shall be my future?" Whereupon the sage blessed her: "My copulation with you won't sully your maidenhood. You shall be a most comely and desireable maiden. It is the will of the Providence which made me desire you even though I have withstood the advances of most beautiful damsels from the heaven and earth. And as far as my seed impregnating you is concerned, you shall beget a brilliant and intelligent son whose rearing up won't be the duty of you or your father. Neither his birth would, in any way, cast a dent upon your untouched maidenhood."

Having assured her, the sage Parashar lovingly copulated with her. After that he took a dip in the river Yamuna and left to complete his remaining pilgrimage. At due time, after his diparture, the girl gave birth to a robust and brilliant son on an island who later on came to be known as Vyas Dweepayan (the Vyas born on an island). As soon as he was born he was intelligent enough to beg permission from his mother to perform penance with the assurance that he would return to his mother whenever she wished so. It was he who crossed the sphere of all the Vedic knowledge like a diameter [Hence the term Vedavyas] It was he who wrote, rewrote, edited and compiled all the sacred text and created the magnum opns : the Mahabharat'. Since that woman who emanated fish like smell was Satyavati. Vyas also came to he known as Satyavati's son. Also, owing to his dark complexion, he was called Krishna (dark) Dweipayan (born on an island)

Shantanu's Marriage

When Soota Ji concluded this story, the sages listening to him asked: "How Satyavati came to become Shantanu's wife? Please also relate that incident to us. Soota Ji, then, told this story.

"In the family of Ikshavaku, there was a very pious and religious minded king called Mahamisha. He was very noble and loved his subjects dearly. He completed many Ashwamedha Yagya and eventually got a berth in the heaven after death.

Once in the Gods' assembly when the blowing wind partially removed Ganga's clothes, this king looked lecherously at the divine lady. The Creator Brahma was angry at his impertinence and cursed him as well as Ganga: "You both should descend to the earth straight away as you lack in the divine etiquette." So, in his next birth, that king Mahamisha was born as king Shantanu of Hastinapur who eventually married none other but Ganga, the river in her mortal form.

While telling the details about Bheeshma's birth, Soota ji said: "O Brahmans! Once the Basus[1] with their wives happened to reach sage Vashishtha's hermitage. The wife of the Basu "Dyo' couldn't help stealing the Nandini cow of the sage whose milk was just like nectar. The wife of Dyo wanted her mortal lady friend taste a little of that milk. So, quietly she stole the cow. When the Basus had visited Vashishtha's hermitage, the sage was absent. As he returned to his hermitage and learnt about the theft of his favourite cow, with his yogic powers he learnt about the culprit. He was so angry that he cursed all the eight Basus that they would have to leave the heaven and stay on the earth. However when all the Basus came and requested that for one of them committing a crime all of them shouldn't be punished, the sage modified his curse by saying :"the other seven would return to heaven as soon as they get birth on the earth, but Dyo Basu will have to remain on the earth for a pretty long time. Also since be couldn't check his wife from committing the theft, he will remain unmarried during his stay on the earth as well."

The Basus then further requested: "O Sage, we are used to surviving a divine diet. But when in the human form, how would be getting our due food?" Vashishtha then assured them that it was through Ganga's womb that they would get their mortal birth and hence their divine diet would continue to be available to them.

It is said that once King Pratip of Hastinapur was having bath in a river when he found a small girl pirched on his knees. The king said: "You are too small to be my wife However, in case I get a son by God's grace I'd accept you as my daughter-in-law. That small girl was no one else but the river Ganga in that form who disappeared after revealing her identity.

As the Providence had willed it, Pratip got a son named Shantanu. As the boy came of age, Pratip made him the king of Hastinapur and retired to forest. However, before departing he told his son: "I'm committed to making Ganga as my daughter-in-law. When you meet her, you should marry her!"

---

1. Custodian of the divine offlunce, a kind of devi-devine existence

Once it so happened that when Shantanu was hunting on the banks of the river Ganga, he spotted a grownup girl. Shantanu was captivated by her charm and he proposed to marry that girl. But she put forth her conditions:

1. That she would be free to roam about any where she wanted.
2. That the king would never check her movements.
3. In case the king did, she would be free to desert him.

The king readily accepted the condition and then they were happily married.

Bheeshma's Birth

Following their marriage, every son that they begot was drowned by mother in the river Ganga. Bound by the conditions, Shantanu couldn't stop his wife for doing so. This happened seven times and Shantanu lost his seven sons. But, as she was about to commit the same act the eighth time, Shantanu couldn't control himself. He said: "O heart-less mother! Why are you killing your infant sons? Now I won't let you commit it the same beinous act this time. I won't let my eighth son be drowned at all." Saying so, Shantanu snatched his eighth child from Ganga's fold. Then Ganga told him all about the cursed she carried alongwith them for their mortal birth as also about sage Vashishtha's curse to Basu. She departed, since the condition for her stay was broken, but assuring Shantanu: "Your this son will be renowned person all over the world. But I would rear him up till he is 16 and then I'd give him back to you for ever. This I say only for the welfare of our son."

Getting all the details Shantanu was pacified and realising the sense in Ganga, the mother, rearing up the son from infancy to adolescence, he let her depart with their 8th son on her lap.

Fulfilling her promise Ganga looked after the boy named 'Devavrat' well, making him get best education. It was the renowned sage Parashuram who taught him the martial arts and archery. At due time Ganga brought the boy back to Shantanu. He was delighted to have such a brilliant son, well read and an expert in archery. Since Devvrat was Ganga's son, he was known as

Gangeya as well. As the boy grew into a young man with infinite promise, Shantanu entrusted all state duties to him and engaged in his favourate pastime:hunting.

Bheeshma's Terrible vow

Once while chasing the beasts, Shantanu happeped to reach the bank of the river Yamuna. As he reached there he felt an extremely pleasant heavenly fragrance spreading all around which appeared much more intoxicating than all the perfumes of musk, bela and other flowers put together. Searching for the source of that fragrance he reached close to an extremely beautiful girl. But she has ill-clad and had dishevelled hair. Yet her body was the source that was emanating that maddening fragrance. Seeing her loveliness, fragrance but hizarre clothes he couldn't decipher as to which race she belonged to: was she a Gandharva or Nag-girl or a divine danseuse gone astray on her path?

As he reached closer Shantanu sought her introduction. Then the girl said. "I'm a Dheevar (low-cast) girl, a daughter of the boat man here and my profession is rowing boat across the Yamuna to help the passer by cross this mighty stream."

Shantanu had madly fallen in love to her and he was prepared to have that girl at any cost. Calling himself to be an unmarried person the aged king demanded the girl's hand in marriage. But that girl, who was no one else but Satyavati, replied in a measured tone: "O King! I am not that independent to take the dicision concering my marriage. Hence the properiety demands your giving your this offer-to marry me-to my father. In case he agrees, I'll have no objections." Getting this suggestion, Shantanu broached this topic before Nishaad, the father of Satyavati. He offered to give a large sum of money in the exchange for receiving the girl as alms in marriage, called KANYADAAN. Knowing Shantanu's desire the wise and shrewd Nishad said: "O King! It will be my great good fortune if a king like you desires to marry my daughter. But before that you must give your word that only your son begotten by her would be the ruler after you."

Now this was a hard condition. Although he didn't disclose that he had a grown up son, Devavrat, yet remembering him, the king was greatly perturbed. How could he have neglected his dear Gangeya?

Dejected he returned to Hastinapur. But the memory of Satyavati's captivating charms made him quite restless. He almost forgave his food and other kingly duties as well. He remained norose and forlorn, lost in his melancholic reverie. Seeing his father in mech a sullen and sorry mood, Devavrat requested him to reveal the reason of his melancholy. He said: "O Sire! It has been our tradition in which sons would do anything to keep their father happy. The example of Lord Rama and Parashuram are there to vindicate my point. Please don't think I will be found wanting in this traditon as well. I can do any thing; sacrifice even the most disireable happiness to see you happy. Just tell me as to what can make you happy again."

Shantanu said: "My Beloved! I am glad to know your feelings about me. But my worry is: you are my only son. Should any thing untoward befall you, who will be there to perform my last-rites and give me post-mortem oblation?" Devavrat was rather amazed to know this most illogical cause of his father's worry. He deduced that "Father is hiding the real cause of his worry from me. I must find out from his ministers and charioteers who accompanied him in his last hunting expedition, since after that only he has fallen in this state of grief and melancholy."

When he kept on enquiring, he soon learnt the real cause of his father's worry. Having learnt it, Devavrat straight away went to that Nishaad and assured him on behalf of his father that Satyavati's son would be Hastinapur's ruler after Shantanu. But that cunning Nishaad said: "Of cource it is a praiseworthy sacrifice on your part for your father's sake . But you might renounce your right upon the throne, what would happen when your son demands his right over it?" Then Devavrat took a terrible vow. "O Nishaad! Rest assured that there will be no such contestant. Here and now I take the vow that I shall never marry. This way I will never get any son and now your apprehension should be nullified." All those who were present there praised Devavrat. When Shantanu heard about it, he was greatly touched by Devavrat's affection for him. He called Devavrat close to him and said: "Since you have taken such a terrible vow, you will be called Bheeshma henceforth. And out of sheer gratitude I grant you two boons: You will be remembred by our entire race for ever and no Hindu son's oblation to his departed ancestor would be complete unless it is precided by a libation to you. Secondly, you will meet your death only when you yourself desire your end."

Then the boat man readily consented for Satyavati's merriage with Shantanu. Satyavati got two sons from this union. Chitrangada and Vichitraveerya. But both died untimely, leaving the throne of Hastinapur with no heir appearent. At last Satyavati made Vyas produce two son from her widowed daughter-in-law through the provision of Niyoga which bore scriptural sanction But while Ambika fainted seeing Vedavyas unclad and hence fearsome, which resulted in her bearing a blind son called Dhritarashtra, Ambalika cowered in fear when Vedavyas came close and hence she produced a son perpetually affected with excess of the yellow pigment which made his complexion yellow. Hence he was called Pandu (literally meaning yellow) Only when Vedavyas copulated with a palace-maid, at Satyavati's behest, that he really enjoyed the act since that maid was adapt in sexual poses. This union, consequently, produced Vidur who was the most learned and wise fellow in the entire Kuru clan. By a unanimous dicision of the clan, Pandu was made the king and Vidur, the minister. Dhritarashtra was not considered for the kingship owing to his blindness. Bheeshma, later on, made Dhritarashtra marry the princes of Gandhar-land, named Gandhari and another lady called Suhali. Dhritarashtra got 100 sons from Gandhari and one Kantiman from Suhali, While the names of Pandu's wives were Kunti, the princes from Shoorseni Pradesh, and Madri from Madra Pradesh who respectively begot three sons, and two sons. [There is an interesting legend woven into the birth of Pandu's sons which is given below.]

Pandavas' Birth

Once King Pandu had gone for hunting with his wives and accidentally he happened to shoot dead a sage who, in the form of a deer, was capulating with his wife, also in a doe-form. Before dying the sage cursed Pandu that if he ever tried to have sex with his wife, he would die instantly. Once Pandu couldn't resist and forced his wife Madri to have sex with him. Consequently, he died due to the effect of the sage's curse. Now the kingdom of Hastinapur was again left without a king. But before Pandu's death, Kunti had disclosed him about formula she had recieved from the Sun God who had produced a son, Karna, from him when she was unmarried. Although she deserted her that son out of fear for social calumny yet finding Pandu incapable of producing a son from his espouses, she suggested using the formula. Pandu, realising the necessity of having a son, consented. Then Kunti produced Yudhishtir from her union with Dharmaraja, Bhim from her union with the Wind-God and Arjuna from her union with Indra, king of Gods. Kunti also revealed this secret formula for getting a son with the divine union to Madri as well who also got two sons by invoking the divine phyisicions pair- the Ashwini Kumars. After Pandu's death, Kunti and Madri with their five sons were to go back to Hastinapur but Madri decided to end her existence on the pyre of her departed husband, entrusting her two sons' custody to Kunti.

As she reached the capital some persons objected her and Madri getting sons from the divine union, but Kunti,, citing examples from the family pacified them. Meanwhile Dhritarashtra, who was also acting as the regent of the kingdom, had his over ambitious son, Duryodhan eyeing courteously at the throne. This caused much heart-burning among the Kauravas (son of Dhritarashtra) and the Paandavas which eventually led to the famous war of Mahabharat, as is known to every one.

Continuing the narration, Soota Ji said: "O noble brahmans! The third Pandawa Arjuna got married to Subhadra, the sister of Lord Krishna who produced Abhimanyu. Although in the war all the Kauravas and the discendants of the Pandavas were slain, the Pandava's lineage could continue owing to Abhimanyu's wife Uttara carrying seed of Abhimanyu in her womb. She had produced a still-born child who was revived to life by Lord Krishna's efforts. He was called Parikshit. When the Pandavas retired to the Himalayas, they made Parikshit the King. The Pandavas later on quitted their mortal coil in the Himalayas. In fact, Parikshit was the sole survivor of the entire Kuru's clam.

Parikshit And Janmejaya

Parikshit ruled over the earth for 60 years. By that time Kaliyug had made its advent on the earth. Owing to this effect, once Parikshit went for hunting. On the way to the jungle he went astray, leaving all his ministers and soldiers behind. Feeling extremely thirsty he happened to find a lovely hut in which an ascetic was sitting lost in his meditation. Parikshit repeatelly asked him to get him some water but the ascetic kept mum. At last Parikshit lost his temper and put a dead serpent lying closely round the ascetic's neck in anger. Still the ascetic kept quite. Although the king (Parikshit) returned home subsequently, the ascetic's son was a powerful Yogi. When he returned to find his father so contemptuously insulted, naming Parikshit, he cursed that with in seven nights he would be fatally bitten by a deadly snake called Takshak.

When Parikshit learnt about this curse, he consulted his minister to have a totally snakeproof chamber constructed and when the arrangement was made he began to dwell in it. In his kingdom there was also a seer Kashyap who was an expert in nullifying the toxic effect of the snake bite. Hearing about Takshak's determination to fatally bite Parikdhit, he left home to go to Hastinapur and help his king against Takshak's threat. Kashyap was in fact a poor man. He had started his journey for Hastinapur with the intention of earning much gold from the king as a reward to his expertise in detoxifying the snake bite. As the luck would have it, he met Takshak in disguise on the way. When Takshak learnt about his intentions, he revealed himself and said: "Let me test your expertise. I am Takshak. Now I bite this tree." As soon as he bit at the stem of the tree, that verdant tree became a leaf-less dry piece of wood owing to the high toxicity of the venom. But Kashyap immediately sprinkled some water over it, charging with his Mantra and it was green again. Takshak realised that he might not succed in killing Parikshit. So he offered large amount of gold coins to that poor brahman who returned, demming this course of event to be the will of the destiny.

Now Takshak proceeded to Hastinapur. And despite all the security, he managed to become as small as an insect and hide himself among the fruits to be taken into the palace for Parikshit's consumption. As he reached near Parikshit, Takshak regained his form and fatally bit Parikshit who died instently.

After Parikshit's death, his son, Janmejaya ascended to the throne of Hastinapur. One day sage Utank, who was also distressed by Takshak, came to the king and reminded the latter about Takshak killing his father. He inspired Janmejaya enough to make the king perform a Yagya to end the species of snakes.

The Yagya duly started and with every oblation poured into the holy fire, snakes began to fall into the pit to be consumed by fire. This 'Sarpa-Yagya' created a dread among all the species of serpents. So much so that their leader, Takshak, was so much terrified that he sought the divine king Indra's protection. Indra asked him to sit glued to his divine throne. But the power of the Mantras chanted by Utanka and sages made even Indra's throne descend to the holy fire pit. At that very moment, the sage Aasteeka who was related to the snakes, used his counter Mantras to stabilise Indra's throne mid-way. Then Aasteeka impressed upon Janmejaya to end the holocaust since it was grossly unfair to exterminate a full species in vergeance to punish his father's killer. Other sages also intervened and eventually that dreadful Yagya was stopped. Ever since then Takshaka assured all beings that a mere utterance of the name 'Asteeka' would prevent any snake from biting anyone. He also gave the ruling that if any snake broke this rule, it would have its head broken into a hundred peaces.

Having done so, Janmejaya asked Vyas Ji as to how his father's soul could be liberated from the stigma of insulting a brahman. Vyas Ji said: "On his behalf you must listen to the Blessed Devi Bhagwat Purana. After Shukadeva you would be the second person to listen to this supremely secret and efficacious Purana giving instant liberation from all kinds of bondages."

❑❑

THIRD CHAPTER.......

Janmejaya asked the Great Sage (Vedavyas): "O Sire! Please enlighten me about the Origin, form and the Great Goddess' hold upon the entire creation Vyas Ji replied that once the same question he had enquired from Narad about as to who was the Originator of this entire universe since there were many legends which were quite confusing. Narad also said: "Dear! I was also confused about it. Then I had asked my Creator, Brahma, as to who was the top deity among all and how this entire world came to be created."

The Story of The Beginning

He replied: "It is a difficult question. Even then I would try to answer to the best of my ability. This question can be answered only by some one who is totally impartial and free from all prejudices and predilections."

Then he told me this story. Once during the Great Pralaya (Dissolution) the whole earth was under water. Then I was born through a lotus. At that time I could not spot any planet, contellations or stars even. Seated on the lotus I kept on broading over that Primal energy that brought me into existance. I also wanted to know the root of my base, the earth. But despite having made efforts for about a 1000 years I couldn't hit the base. At that point of time I heard a divine voice asking me to do penance. I did so for yet another 1000 years. Then I was ordered: "Create" I was surprised as to how I was supposed to create. At that very moment I spotted the demons Madhu and Kaitabh. In the fear of them I began to descend holding the lotus stem. There I espied Lord Vishnu adorned with the oonch-shell, discuss, a mace and a lotus with a garland of flower round his neck.

But he was asleep on his bed made from the serpent Shesh's coil. It was then that in the great dread I remembered the Supreme Goddess and she appeared before me in her super-human form, emerging from the body of Lord Vishnu. Then I saw Vishnu fighting with those demons, having been awaken due to that Goddess's inspiration. He fought for long and eventually succeeded in slaying those demons. At that time Lord Shiv also appeared there. Then we formed the Superme Trinity and worshipped the Goddess in total unison.

Blessing we three, the Goddess said: "Now since both the demons:Madhu and Kaitabh have been slain by my wish, you three must devote youself in creation, sustenance and distruction of the world" Whereupon I said to the Goddess: "O Mother! There is nothing but water everywhere. How can I start the process of creation?"

Then the Goddess beckoned mysteriously and there appeared an aerial vehicle (Vimana) sitting in which we three reached a beautiful spot replete with lotus-filled ponds, picturesque forests, rivers and mountains. On enquiry we learnt that it was heaven (Swargalok) where we met the divine lord Indra, the divine danseses, the Gandharvas and the Kinnars from there the velicle took us to Brahm's (my) loka where I was seen seated on a lotus flower with Brahmajis chanting Vedic Hymns.

The dwellers of the Brahma-loka (Brahma's realm) were surprised to see me; they were bewildered as to where from had arrived there another Brahma? Then the vehicle took us a beautiful mount called Kailash Parvat. Lord Shiv was sitting there on the peak amidst his hencemen. Both the Shivs were surprised seeing each other. Finally the vehicle took us to Vaikuntha (Vishnu's realm) There, reclining on the bed of the Shesh serpent coil was Vishnu with Lakshmi massaging his feet. Now Vishnu-who was with us-was also startled. Leaving that place too, the Vehicle flew to an indescribably enchanting place having gem bedecked thrones with a grand throne in between having the Super Goddess radiating all the ten directions with her dazzling glow. All Gods including Indra, Vishnu, Shiv and myself were encircling the grand throne. But we were unable to recognise that Super Existence."

While narrating this Brahma said: "Dear son! Realising my ardent wish Vishnu said: 'Brahma!' Now I remember. When in a child's form I was sleeping on a leaf on a banyan, it was this Goddess who protected me. If you recollect even in the Ocean we had seen her! We are really very fortunate to have been blessed with her Darshan. Our penance and prayers have received their fruition in the form of the Super Devi (Goddess) appearing before us.

"We had stayed there for about a 100 years. While we were constantly hymning her glories, one day she told me that like the object and the shadows we are no different from her in any way." So, You three go and look after the creation." While I was entrusted with the job of creation, Vishnu with its sustenance and Shiv with its distruction."

Referring about this incident Vyas Ji told Janmejaya : "During that time Narad Ji made it clear before me that anyone devotedly chanting her name, the Mother of Universe (Jagadamba) always shed her grace upon the devotee. Once a brahman Satyavrata chanted: "Em heem kleem Chaamundaya namaha". Even when he chanted 'Em' the Mother had provided him total riddanace from fear." And that Brahmana also earned the epithet of Kaviraj (Lord of Poets) by chanting this mantra. This episode is well known to every one."

But Janmejaya wanted to know this episode in details. Vyas Ji obliged him by narrating the full story. He told him this:

Once Vyas Ji happened to reach in the cource of his pilgrimage Nemisharanya. There, when he found Lomash sage and the sage Jamadagni busy in an intellectual discussion, he stayed back there. Jamadagni then asked Lomash Ji: "O Great Sage! Who among all the deities is most adorable?"

"The Supreme Goddess Jagadamba" is the origin of all the Gods and hence most adorable. In this connection I narrate you one incident. Once there lived a famous brahman named Devadatta in the kindgom of Kaushal. He had all the virtues but he was issueless. In order to get one son, he invited the learned sages on the bank of the river Tamasoa to do the 'Putreshthi Yagya'. In that Yagya was also present the sage Gobhil who used to mispronounce a little the hymns. When he was rebuked for this mistake he became angry and cursed Devadutta that" You would get a stupid son". But when Devadutta requested him repeatedly he made a modification in his curse that "Your son, though born stupid, would become an erudite scholar later on."

Utathya's Englightenment

At due time the brahman's wife delivered a son, who was named Utathya. The sacred thread ceremony was completed when he became 8 years old. Then he was sent to a school but dispite valiant efforts made by his teachers he failed to learn any thing. Even when he had become 12 years of age he continued to be a dunce. So in the entire region he became notorious enough for his folishness. He was blank in all the rituals despite being a brahman. But he had one good quality that he never damaged anybody's interest. Nor he would ever tell a lie. However, becoming a butt of ridicule from every one, he was so much frustrated that he started dwelling quietly on the bank of the river Ganga.

One day when he was sitting beneath a tree he happened to find a deer, wounded by a hunter's arrow, close to him. Out of pity he hid the wounded deer in his hut. Meanwhile, that hunter came to Utathya and asked about that deer. "O sage!, said the hunter," it is my profession to catch hold of my preys. Please tell me as to where my prey might be." Now Utathya was in a great fix. For if he spoke truth, the deer seeking his shelter would be slain and if not that he would be committing a felony he never committed in his lfie. Then he sought shelter in the Goddess's refuge. And immediately his eloquent powers became fully charged. He told the hunter in a poetic language: "How can I tell about that deer? For the senses that saw her can't speak and those that speak couldn't have seen him" Hearing this confusing answer the hunter went back. But that made Satyavrata again intelligent and learned. Following this incident he came to be renowned as Satyavrata, the scholar who latter on created the famous 'Beeja Mantra' in the honour of the Super Godess."

Concluding the narration Vyas Ji told Janmejaya: "No other deity responds to the genuine prayers as quickly as the Goddess Jagadamba does. Hence she is the most adorable Deity."

Continuing the narration again, Vyas Ji attempted to describe the glorious antiquity of the Supreme Goddess. When Brahma, Vishnu and Mahesh (Shiv) saw the whole creation, they were amazed. Then they were asked to create, maintain and destroy it the same was by the Goddess. Following the commands the Triumvirate created the realms; each according to his liking. Brahma created the first pair of humans. Manu from his right part and Shataroopa from his left part. When the world was created on the advice of Vishnu a thanks-giving Yagya was performed to display the divinities gratitude towards the Great Goddess. Delighted by the worship the Goddess blessed Vishnu to be most important and potent deity among all the divinites. She also advised him to incarnate on the earth whenever villains thrived and the noble got enervated. "Your primary duty shall be to uphold the righeous order for which you may be required to go on to the earth in a variety of forms. But the energy given to you should never be misused. You should deem yourself to be my instrument to follow the destined course." After this the Goddess disappeared and thanking all Vishnu bade adien to all the Gods."

Vyas Ji said that this was the reason why Vishnu was declared to be the most potent God since he has the backing of the Primal Power.

Deteching the unquenchable curiosity in Janmejaya, Vyas Ji said: "Now I'd recite to you another episode which highlights the Goddess's glory." Then he narrated this story.

Yudhajit Story

Once there ruled a king Dhrvuasandhi in Ayodhya. He was a noble, righteous and God-fearing ruler. He had two beautiful daughters named Lilavati and Manorama who respectively produced two sons : Subal and Sudarshan, for the King. Once when the King went for hunting he was killed by a beast. Then after due deliberations the ministers chose Sudarshan to ascend to the throne. Meanwhile Manorama's father Veerasen and Lilavati's father Yudhhajit came to Ayodhya to condole for the death of their son-in-law. Yuddhajit questioned the ministers as to why had they appointed the younger prince as the king when the elder one was available. The minister's defended by calling Sudarshan to be more competent and brave than the elder prince, Subal. However, a bitter dispute arose on this issue between the two parties and Yuddhajit happened to kill Veerasen in the duel. When Manorama heard about her father's death she was worried as to who would now protect her son's life. So she consulted the senior minister Vidalla, who advised her to leave the place with her son and she sought shelter at her maternal uncle, Subahu's place. Taking along her precious gems, son, some faithful servants and guided by the trusted minister Vidalla, she left Ayodhya quitly. Unfortunately the caravan was attacked by dacoites on the way who looted all the precious gems that the Queen had. Now, the Queen became almost a pauper. With great difficulty she managed to cross the river Ganga that lay in between and reached the hermitage of sage Bharadwaj. When the sage enquired of her introduction she couldn't speak much in the excessive grief and then Vidalla disclosed the details to the sage.

Meanwhile Yuddhajit was still searching for the absconding Queen and the Prince with the objective of clearing the troubles for his nephews unfettered rule. So he sent his sleuths in every direction. Duly they informed about the fugitive Queen and the Prince's presence in the hermitage of Sage Bhardwaj. Immediately Yuddhajit left for the hermitage. Reaching there he threatened the sage that either he should handover the Queen and the Prince to him or he might forcibly snatch them to his control. The sage warned him, "Don't try to be as fool hardy as sage Vishwamitra was who tried to forcibly usurp sage Vashishtha's incomparable cow called Nandini. In any case, if you want to quit this world untimely, you are most welcome to attack my hermitage and take away the Queen and her son."

Yuddhajit cowered in recollecting that eminence of the Brahma Tej (Spiritual power) and quitely went away. At last Manorama heaved a sigh of relief. She began to stay in that hermitage with her son in a peaceful relief.

Sudershana's Worship

While staying with other disciples of the sage, Sudershan also learnt the Holy Mantra of the Supreme Goddess: "OM EM HEEM KLEEM CHAMUNDAYA NAHAM". But after some time he forgot to pronounce it fully and kept on chanting only the first two words.

But the Gooddess shed her grace on him even though he chanted only one third of the Beej Mantra.

Once the daughter of the Kashi-Ruler, Shashikala happened to see Sudershan in a forest and she was captivated by the prince's charms. She made her friends convey this desire that her parents who, having learnt about their daughter's choice, decided to invite Sudershana to Kashi to participate in the Swayamvar (the bride's selection for the husband fulfilling certain conditions). By this time Sudershan had become quite popular in the region and the main boatman of Shringaverpur, Nishaad, offered to drive his chariot. It was the Devi Bhagwati's will which eventually made the Kashiraj declare Sudarshana to be her daughter's final choice. Yuddhajit was also present in that Swayamvar who called it to be the most heinous insult heaped the invited kings. "Why did you invite all when the choice was made before-hand," he asked the Kashi ruler in his thundering voice. He even advised the Kashi king to reconsider his decision as Sudershan was a coward, he insisted. The ruler of Kashi was some what apprehensive of the other kings under Yuddhajit's leadership who might forcibly make him alter the choice. So he advised Sudarshana and Shashikala to quitly slip out of Kashi. But Sudershana refused: "I have come here inspired by the Great Goddess and I will go back only if She wills so." The Kashi-ruler also endorsed this strategy. Although owing to the Goddess's inspiration, most of the invited kings remained neutral, yet Yuddhajit started the war. Seeing her devotees falling in trouble the Goddess herself came to fight from the side of Sudershana. At last Sudarshana was killed and then Kashiraj duly solemnised his daughter's marriage with Sudarshana. By this time he had become quite renowned and bowing his head alongwith his wife to sage Bhardwaj on way to Ayodhya, he reached his lost capital where he was again duly appointed as the king. During his rule Sudarshana had many temples dedicated to the Goddess made in his kingdom. After many eons, enjoying full life, Sudarshana left for the heaven due to his genuine and single-pointed devotion for the Goddess. It was he who ruled that the Great Goddess must be especially worshipped during every Navaratra.

The Goddess's Ritual Worship

Getting these details Janmejaya was curious about learning the ritual worship of the Goddess during the Navaratri period. Then Vyas Ji told him in details about it. "O King! For the Navaratri falling in the dark fortnight during Sharad ritu (Sept.-Oct.) the advance preparations should be made night from the Moon-less day (Amavasya) itself. A square area of 16 hands length (one hand about 1.5') long and broad duly covered with a canopy should be selected, covered with thin layer of cow-dung paste and soil. The altar should be made at the middle of that area. A devotee of the Goddess, a well-learned brahman, should be invited. On the day one of the lunar fortnight, after ritual cleansings early in the morning, bath should be taken and white, clean, apparels should be worn. Then duly welcoming the brahman folks, the idol of Goddess Jagdamba should be placed and consecrated. Then the earthen pitcher filled with clean water should be installed. This should be followed by the regular worship of the Goddess concluded with singing of the hymns glorifying the deeds of the Goddess. The virgins of different ages are to be duly worshipped: On first day a two year old; on second day a three year old, on third day a four year old girl and so on (till for the 9th day). These worships yield great benefit for the worshipers right from ending of all mental physical affiction to recieving all kinds of physical, economic and spiritual wealth. Concluding the narration Vyas Ji said that "When Rama, the Great Lord, worshipped the Goddess, he could win back his lost wife Sita."

When Janmejaya showed his curiosity to know about how Rama won back her wife Sita by the virtue of his performing a very devoted worship of the Great Goddess, the sage, narrated him the entire Rama-Katha. It was on the eighth day of his worship of the Goddess that she appered before him and blessed him with reunion with his seperated wife. Eventually Rama defeated Ravan and triumphantly returned to Ayodhya.

◻◻

FOURTH CHAPTER.......

Hearing Rama's Story, Janmejaya said: "O supremely learned sage! Now I am curious to learn the Krishna-Charita from your blessed mouth. I feel that the Character of Krishna is full of self contradictions. Please tell me about his life story so that my doubt could be removed."

The Causes of the Krishna Incarnation

Referring about this dialogue, Soota Ji said. "Answering to Janmejaya's query, Sage Vyas said: 'One can not escape the cousequence of any action. Even the Gods can't, let alone the mortals. In fact even the Gods are not beyond prejudices and predilections which make them commit indiscreet actions. As a matter of fact, no body can even remain actionless having come into an existence but once the action is committed no one, not even the mighty Gods, can escape facing their cousequences." Then he discussed the various reasons behind Lord Vishnu repeatedly incarnating himself or the conditions that would compel him to come to the earth, while dilating upon the causes that made Vishnu come as Krishna.

One of the reasons was Sage Kashyapa receiving a curse from Varuna. Once the sage forcibly took Varuna's cow away for performing a Yagya. But he refused to return the cow even though Varuna persisted for it later on. Then Varuna complained about the sage's misbehaviour to the Creator, Brahma, and also told him that, enraged by the sage's this unseemly conduct, he had cursed the sage that he would have to descend on to the Earth with his two wives: Aditi and Diti. Brahma, then, summoned Kashyapa who was still adamant for not returning the cow. This made Brahma eventually support Varuna and endorsing his curse. That was the reason why the sage had to take birth on the Earth as Vasudeva with his two wives.

Sage Kashyapa's both wives: Aditi and Diti were the daughters of Daksha Prajapati. Aditi produced a brilliant son, Indra, from Kashyapa's seed. When Diti demanded a similar son, Kashyapa asked her to follow a vigorous schedule involving many stern conditions of living like sleeping on the floor, ritually cleaning her mouth before ritiring for the day. After getting pregnant Diti started following all these instructions religiously and soon her body glowed, giving the symptom of her conceiving a brilliant, Indra-like son. This made Aditi jealous. She thought lest she should beget a mightier son that even Indra. So she asked her son Indra to fail her co-wife's disigns. The obedient son, Indra, accepted the job to please his mother.

One day he quietly went to Diti and lovingly started massaging her feet. Diti, being pregnant, felt great comfort and in lethargy she fell asleep without even washing her mouth. Indra, meanwhile, seized his opportunity and entered her womb assuming a tiny form, to cut in seven pices the growing embryo. When the embryo lamented in pain he said "Ma rodi (don't weep)!" And to assure the success of his mission, Indra further cut the each of the seven pieces seven times again. With the result-there were now 49 pieces who were eventually born as 49 Marutas. However, when Indra accomplished his heinous mission, Diti got up in pain and realised what Indra had done at Aditi's behest. She cursed her co-wife Aditi that like she had made her embryo divided in the multiples of seven, On the earth she would have to produce seven dead sons. So in Dwapar she was born as Devaki, the wife of Vasudeva who had to see her seven sons killed by Kansa exactly at the time they were born.

While dilating upon yet another reason for Krishna's incarnation Vedavyas said to Janmejaya. :"O King! Daksha Prajapati married his ten daughters to Dharma (Dharmaraja) and their union produced many sons as well. Two of them were Nara and Narayana who were of very pious nature and as they came of age they left for Badrinath to perform a vigorous penance. They did it so devotedly that Indra was worried lest they should become as much powerful as to snatch his divine throne. With the result he himself reached Badrikashrama (Badrinath) astride his pet vehicle, the Elephant Eiravat, and started hurling weapons at the meditating duo of the sages. But he couldn't disturb their concentration. At last, he returned to heaven and sought services of Kamadeva-the Love-God. "Take along with you all of your love engendering paraphernalia and the most comely dauseuses from my capital and disturb those two ascetics' penance. Else they would dethrone me."

As the love-God reached the indicated destination and created the love-engendering atmosphere of gardens laden with fragrant flowers, to his utter surprise to find the ascetics totally unperturbed. Having failed in its attempt, he asked the Apsaras (Divine Dausense) to display their litillating magic. The Apsaras tried all tricks up their sleeves to attract the ascetics but to no avail. However, getting engaged realising the divine-lord Indra's intentions, Nara hit his knee powerfully with his hand. And lo and behold. There emerged the beautiful woman , the renowned Apsara, Urvashi, with her uncountable maids. Then Nara told Kama: "Take her to your Lord Indra. Tell him that never make such attempt before the genuine ascetics for we can produce in a flick more beautiful dames then he has in his entire divine harem!"

Although Kama returned but most of the Apsaras along with the created other dames refused to go to heaven. They requested the ascetics.

"Don't send us back, Lord! We don't want to go. If you accept us as your wives we shall deem our existence successful."

This seducing offer from the Apsaras worried Narayana.. "Their stay here might really disturb our concentration." Then he advised Nara to shed anger "which is the supposed to be a deadlier enemy of our concentration than the amorous feeling of love." Then he revealed that once this anger had disturbed their penance when Narayan had assumed the form of Nrisimha to slay Hiranyakashyapa.

Prahlad And Nara-Narayana

Janmejaya was curious. "O Great Sage Vyas! Please narrate to me this full episode. How could the renowned devotee Prahlad take up cudgels against the exalted sages Nara and Narayana?"

Vyas Ji obliged him by telling this story. After the wicked king Hiranyakashyapu was slain, his son, Prahlad was made the king of the Asuras. Now, he was an ardent devotee of Lord Vishnu. Once he was sitting in his court, there arrived the exalted sage Chyavvan. After duly welcoming the sage and asked: "O Great Sage! Which is that teerth (Holy spot) going where one may get the Darshana of the Blessed Lord Vishnu." The sage then dilated upon the fact and said that one with clean heart might see such a pilgrim centre every where. "However, those with clean heart should go to Nemisharnya where they may visualise the Blessed Lord quite cleanly."

Getting this hint, Prahlad with his entourage reached Nemisharnya. There he saw an unusual spectacle. While one ascetic with the grey, matted hair was lost in his meditation, yet another with very keen arrows and bow was standing guard to the first one. Prahlad asked the other one as to why he was there with the arrows and bow since that was the ascetics zone. Whereupon Nara said: "An undisturbed meditation cares not for even an idota of any kind of disturbance. But since you are an Asura you might, perhaps, not understand such subtleties. So you better go away." Prahlad was some what annoyed at this disdainful reply. He said: "Okay! Since you call me to be an Asura incapable of understanding the fine nuances of meditation. I challange you: Either you remove all these weapons from this peace zone or fight with me a regular war." This was enough for the two ascetics to feel charged with indignation. They began to rain arrows over Prahlad and his army. Prahlad began to face them. Soon this confrontation became a full fledged war with Asuras coming to help Prahlad and Gods to Nara and Narayana. This war continued for many days. At last Prahlad privately requested his chosen deity Vishnu to intervene and have the dispute resolved. The Blessed Lord advised him: "Nara-Narayana are my partial form. You can't defeat them. So it would be better if you retreat gracefully."

Heeding Vishnu's advice Prahlad returned and the two ascetics continued with their meditation. Saying so, the sage Vedavyas opined : "O King! remember that anger and arrogance at times appear more deadly enemies of man than even the lecherous love. A little anger can erode your years of meditation and deprive you of its great merits. For in anger man loses his discretion and the sense of discernment ."

Continuing the story he said :"Anger had given a great set-back to both the sage's meditative power as well. It is anger which disturbs the composure of even the saints more than any other sentiment. Hence one should always stay cool. The anger that the ascetic-duo had shown in Prahlad's case had made them start their effort again. It is, however, not easy to control one's anger."

Sage Bhrigu And Vishnu

Then citing the example of the Sage Bhrigu, Vedavyas told Janmejaya about how this great sage had become so mad in his anger that he even cursed the Blessed Lord Vishnu, saying :"You will have to be born in the lowly species and suffer agony, grief and privation." Janmejaya then wished knowing about the entire episode and Vyas obliged him by narrating the following story.

When Prahlad's grandson Kalki became the Asura king he was defeated by the Gods. Then the demon host sought advice from their Guru, Shukracharya who boosted their morale enough to make them return to the battle field. But the demons were defeated again. This time they reached near their Guru crying in pain and agony. The Guru asked them to seek advice from Lord Shiv. "But you all must develop power through penance to take on the Gods. Meanwhile I would consult the great God Shankar." The demons went away to meditate.

When Shukracharya sought Lord Shankar's advice, despite his desiring no welfare of the demons, out of his simple nature he happened to disclose a secret though difficult 'Sadhana' to Shukra. The demons Guru began to do penance in accordance with Lord Shiv's instructions. As the Guru began to succeed in his Sadhana, the demons felt powerful enough to attack the Gods again. But again they were defeated. Then the demons rushed to the Guru's hermitage who was not present there; only his wife, the Gurumata, was there. Meanwhile, chasing the demons the Gods also reached there. The Guru's wife asked them not to kill those demons. But the Gods didn't care for her order. Seeing this she invoked sleep and made all the Gods fall fast asleep. Only Vishnu remained beyond the sleep's effect. He quietly took his brother Indra away and carried him to the safety of heavens.

The Guru's wife though chased them, yet Indra, wide awake by then, asked her not to kill them. Vishnu, however, was now quite angry and he used his discus to hack off Shukracharya's wife's head. This made the Gods delighted but now the stigma of killing a woman was attached to Vishnu's name.

When a sage Bhrigu learnt about Vishnu killing a woman, he was enraged. After all Shukracharya's wife was a brahman woman. He cursed Vishnu that owing to his this evil deed he would have to take birth in lonely and sub-human species as well. That was why he had to incarnate himself as the Boar, the Tortoise and Fish.

Continuig the tale, Sage Vyas said: "Although Bhrigu revived that woman, the God chief Indra, wasn't satisfied and he desputised his daughter, Jayanti, to disturb Shukracharya's penance. But impressed by Shukra's devotion and priestly awe, instead of showing her sexual charms to disturb him, she began to serve him as a faithful maid. She saw to it that Shukracharya faced no problem in any of the seasons. At last Shukracharya's mission was successful and he recieved the due blessings from Lord Shankar.

Then Shukracharya enquired in details about the woman who so faithfully served him. Jayanti disclosed her identity without any deceitful trick.

She told that she was Indra's daughter, Jayanti. Satisfied with her devoted service and truthfulness Shukra asked her to get any boon she might desire. She said: "O Lord! I want you to marry me and enjoy nuptial bliss for ten years invisibly. Shukracharya said: "So be it" And making her and he invisible they began to enjoy their nuptial bliss in secrecy.

Meanwhile, Indra told Brihaspati all that his daughter had accomplished. Getting this information, Brihaspati (or Vrihaspati) adopted the demon-Guru Shukracharya's form and went to the place where the demons were meditating. The demons thought him to be their real Guru and they lovingly welcomed him with due respect. The divine Guru in disguise managed to overwhelm the demons by his good conduct. As they fell under the false Guru's influence that Guru (in reality the divine Guru Vrihaspati) initiated them in a different faith which deemed all material possessions to be useless and that life itself a burden and the earlier it was got rid of the better[1]. With the result all the demons became indifferent to getting back their due rights from the Gods.

Meanwhile, the term of living with Jayanti of Shukracharya drew to a close and then Shukracharya begged leave for returning to his demon-realm which Jayanti readily allowed. When he reached to his disciples the demons, he found them totally indifferent to material possessions. They even tried to throw real Shukra out as they believed Vrahaspati, the impostor, to be the real Shukra. Shukra, realising the intention of the divine Guru asked the demons not to learn to what ever he (Brihaspati) said but they refused. Then Shukra cursed them that soon their race would perish.

Meanwhile Vrihaspati returned to heaven and apprised Indra about his mission's success. In the mean time the demons also realised as to how Vrihaspati had duped them. They went to Shukra, requesting him to dilute his curse upon them. Since he was angry enough upon the Gods and at his behest they attacked them. Gods were unable to stand before the demons charged onslaught. Then on Vishnu and Indra's advice they invoked the Great Goddess. Soon she responded to their prayer and appeared in her four armed form, astride a lion. Shukracharya also realised the Goddess's greatness and he asked the demons to worship her as well. At last with the Goddess's intervention peace prevailed between the warring groups It was decided that the demons would remain in Patal-look (neither realm) and Gods in heaven.

The Sages Naga-Narayana's Promise

When Janmejaya wanted to know as to what happened the divine dausenses' request to the ascetic duo Nara-Narayana, Vyas Ji told him that the ascetics said: "We can't fulfil your desire in this life-However, promise that in Dwapar we shall fullfil your this wish. In Dwapar Age those two were born as Krishna (Narayana) and Nara (Arjuna) and those Apsaras became their wives in that life.

---

1. The tenet is quite close to faith of Jainism

Lord Krishna's Story

Then on Janmejaya desiring to know about the full life story of Lord Krishna from Sage Vyas, the sage narrated the full story upto Krishna slaying Kansa. But Kansa was the son-in-law of Jarasandha, a mighty tyrant, the ruler of Magadha, who with the deadly black demon Kalayavana came charging at Mathura. Although Krishna defeated him as many as 17 times yet getting sick of his attacks, for the safety of Mathura, Krishna decided to leave Mathura bag and baggage with his entire clan. This Yadava race at last settled in Dwarika. Then taking help from Bhim and Arjuna-the Pandavas- Krishna managed to have Jarasandha killed. He also played a trick upon the demon Kalayavana and made him lose his life when the ancient sage Muchukanda cast his fiery gaze upon the demon.

Meanwhile, Krishna's grandson (or the son of Pradyumna-the son of Krishna from Rukmani) was stolen by a demon called Shambarasura. Krishna was very much perturbed and he worshipped the Great Goddess who said: "Worry not, O Krishna! You will get back your grandson after 16 years. Your this grandson then shall himself kill Shambarasura."

Once the daughter of Jambvant, called Jambvati, who was married to Krishna, desired a son from him. In order to fulfil this demand Krishna worshipped long Lord Shiv and the Great Goddess who eventually blessed him that :"From each of your wife you will get 10 sons. For hundred years you will enjoy family pleasure. Then due to the curse on you from sage Durvasa and Gandhari your whole clan will perish. After your quitting your mortal coil your wives would be stolen by the thieves and decoits. This is the destiny and its course cannot be altered."

Hearing this episode in which Krishna had to worship Lard Shiv and the Great Goddess, Janmejaya asked Vyasji: "Sage! Why did Krishna have to worship Lord Shiv and the Goddess. Was he an inferior God in any way?

Vyas said;"No! He was the most potent incarnation of Vishnu. But since he had come in a human body, he was bound by the mortal laws. It was owing to this limitations that he had to suffer curse from Gandhari and Durvasa as well. All Gods who come on to the earth have to follow certain mortal rules. Only those who worship Great Goddess transcend all such mortal or divine limitations." Then Janmejaya wanted to learn more about Great Goddess's glories and Vyas Ji told him the following tale

❏❏

Fifth Chapter.......

Mahishasur's Slaying

Vyas Ji said: "O King! Long ago there was a demon Lord, named Dani[1] who had two sons called Rambh and Karambh. Once they performed a very vigorous penance. As usual Indra was apprehensive of their intentions. He assumed the form of an alligator, entered into water and killed Karambh. Charged with grief and anger Rambh decided to do a massive Yagya and as the final oblation to the holy fire he decided to offer even his head. Seeing his incomperable courage, the fire-God himself appeared and restrained him from committing suicide. Then the God asked him to get the boon he desired most. Rambh requested to get a son invincible by the Gods, men and demons who might also be capable of winning all the three realms. 'So be it', said the God, adding: "Which ever women you copulate with saying this desire shall beget such a son for you."

Getting this boon Rambh saw the Gandharva revelling in a garden with their dames. He also spotted a beautiful Mahishee who agreed to have physical union with him. She concieved from that union.

Subsequently a Mahisha was also captivated by her charm and despite Rambh's opposition he raped that Mahishee. That maddened Mahisha killed Rambh. Seeing that the Gandharvas protected that Mahishee and killed that offender Mahisha. But the Mahishee decided to burn herself to death on the pyre of Rambh. In that fire Mahisha

---

1. It is from this demon that the name 'Danava' is derived which literally means 'of Dani[1].

was also burnt to death. But from that very fire Rambh emerged as the demon 'Raktabeeja' while the Mahishee emerged as the Goddess.

The dreaded demon Mahishasur was the issue of that Mahisha[1] and Rambh. Mahishasur propitiated Brahma as much as to make the deity appear riding the chariot. When the demon asked for imortality Brahma Ji refused saying that in this mortal world this was not possible. Brahma then asked to demon to seek any other boon. Since the demon apprehended no danger from any female in the arrogance of his masculine power, he said: "O Lord! Grant me this boon that I may not be killed by any male." Saying 'so be it' Brahma departed.

Getting this boon of invincibility the demon Mahishasur became extremely arrogant. He challanged the Gods for a duel. The Gods, knowing his powers, panicked and rushed to Brahma, But he expressed his inability to help the Gods and advised them to seek the help of Shiv and Vishnu as well. But Shiv condemned Brahma first for recklessly doling out boons to the undeserving and expressed his inability to help. Vishnu, though sympathised with them, yet said that perhaps he too, might not be able to defeat that demon. While the Gods were seated on the sea-shore despondently, they heard a divine voice saying: "Ye Gods! Shed a fraction of your individual brilliance which I shall adorn when assuning my eight-armed form." So the Gods did and there appreared before them the Super Goddess in her martial form. The Gods hymned her form thus: "O Mother! You have a face lighted with the Moon's grace, long flowing black hair, eyes like fiery balls, the eyebrows as dark grey as the twilight and arched like Kama's bow string. Your teeth are like white lilys and lips a soft flower's petal".

The Gods were delighted to find the Mother of Universe in a murderous mood. Then the Gods gave the best weapon they had. Having backed her with the best of the divine weapons, the Gods reverentually offered their prayers to her, saying:

---

1. Mahishee literally means a buffalo in Sanskrit but here Mahisha and Mahishee or Mahishasur should be deamed as demons capable of adopting the buffalo-form.

"NAMAH SHIVAYEI KALAYANEI SHAWTYEI PUSHTEI NAMO NAMAH
KALYANAM KURU BHO MATAH TRAAHI NO SHATRU TAAPITAAN"

Delighted with the prayers the Goddess mafticked so loudly as to quake all the realms.

When Mahishasur heard this commotion he sent his sleuths and learnt about the Goddess whom he thought to be a mere woman. So he sent his minister Tamrasur with the message: "O Lady! Come and be my Chief Queen" To this the Goddess responded with:" I am born to slay you. You are destined to die at my hands."

Getting this challange Mahishasur sent a huge army with his leutenant Tamrasura but the whole army was destroyed in no time by the Goddess. Tamrasura managed to escape. When Mahisasur consulted his minister they warned the king about taking on a mighty woman since he was destined to die at the hands of a female only. But overruling them, he sent another army to arrest that 'arrogant woman'. In no time his warriors namely Chikshu, Tamrasura, Lohamoosala etc. were slain. Then Mahishasur sent yet another army led by Asilom and Vidaal. Though they fought bravely but eventually all were destroyed by the Goddess. At last Mahishasur came to take on the Goddess in the form of a buffalo. But before that Incomparable Female Existence he couldn't survive. The Goddess made his all tricks unsuccessful. Though he kept on changing his form the Goddess managed to slay him eventually. Mahishasur's death caused panick in their ranks and they fled in her dread. The Goddess protected the Gods and restored the righteous order.

Delighted by hearing the story revealing the Supreme Goddess's terrible, martial form Janmejaya asked the sage Vedavyas: "O Sage! Does the Great Goddess help only the divinities or she cares for even the mortal men as well?" The sage replied: "She, in fact, protects no body in particular. Her prime aim is to maintain and protect righteous order. Whosoever is noble, righteous and just gets protection of the Devi without any distinction what ever. She has been protecting mortal beings many a time. This facet of the Devi's (Goddess's) glory shall be revealed before you clearly when you listen this story."

Surath's Story

Long long ago, during the Swanochisha Manvantar there ruled a very noble King called Surath. Once he happened to be defeated by his enemies, unfortunately. He took this defeat so deep into his heart that he totally lost confidence upon his ministers. One day, riding the horse alone, he left his home to seek his safety and security elsewhere. While he had covered only a little distance he saw a hut of the sage Sumedha. He reached near him and fell flat at his feet in utter supplication, crying 'help me, O sage!' The sage lovingly welcomed him and lifting the king up made him seated on an exalted seat. Asking him to tell more about him Sumedha also enquired the reason of his visit. The King narrated his tale of woe then the sage showed a safe spot and asked the king to stay there for some time. The King felt greatly obliged and began to dwell there. While staying there he happened to meet a Vaishya (trader) called Samadhi who had also suffered at the hands of his trusted persons and family members as the King had. Both, having faced the trouble of similar nature became good friends. However, the question as to why they should have been cheated so cruelly continued to rankle their minds. So one day they proceeded to the sage to know the cause of their falling on such evil days.

The King introduced the trader to the sage and requested the sage as to how they could be redeemed. The sage said: "O King! This whole world is distressed with greed and falsehood. It is instint, however, by the power of the Supreme Goddess without whose inkling nothing transpires here." Then he told them one interesting mythological legend.

Once while searching for a good spot to do their penance both Vishnu and Brahma left their realms. On way they were embroiled into an animated debate as to who between them was greater. While the debate was on, suddenly there appeared in their midst a huge Lingam, followed by a heavenly voice: "He who is able to measure this Linga shall be considered superior between you two." Getting this instruction Brahma started to measure that huge colomn like Lingam from the top while Vishnu started the exercise from the bottom. Brahma soon returned, claiming to have meausred it while Vishnu said he couldn't see the end of it. Since Brahma had lied, Vishnu couldn't believe him. But the insistent Brahma also produced an evidence-a bunch of Ketaki flowers. This made Mahashiva, whose Lingam that, colomn had been, appeared and cursed Brahma that since he had lied he shall never get as much adoration as Shiv or Vishnu would, and he also forbade the use of the Ketaki (Pandamees) flowers in his worship. At that point of time the Goddess made his appearance to settle the dispute among the three main Gods., explaining:" in vain you three quarrel among yourselves for each of you derives your powers from me."

Concluding the narration, the sage Sumedha said: "So, O king you should make your friend also worship the Ultimate Power, the Great Goddess for your redemption. Soon you shall regain your lost kingdom and wealth."

Commenting upon this episode, sage Vyas said to Janmejaya : "So, O King! It is the Supreme Goddess that comes to help and support all mortal and immortal beings provided they stay on the righteous path. Hence the ultimate object of worship should only be she and not anyone else. That is why all Gods and sages worship only Her."

❏❏

SIXTH CHAPTER.......

Janmejaya said to sage Vyas: :O Great Sage! As you just told that the Supreme Goddess is especially kind to her devotees, my curiosity has grown more intense. Would you please recite some other stories to highlight this point."

The sage: "O King! your curiosity is due to your extreme love for the Great Goddess. Now I will narrate you yet another story to make you assess the infinite greatness of the Great Goddess." Then he told this story.

Indra-Vritra Duel

Once when Twashta was the Prajapati (Progenitor) with his great yogic power he got a son called Vishwaroop who was very religious by nature and of a very noble conduct. He had three horns on his head. Following his father's instructions he devotedly continued his vigorous penance to acquire total self-control and concentration. But Indra was jealous of him. He thought him to be performing all these different deeds for achieving his throne. So he sent his Apsaras : Rambha, Menaka, Urvashi, Ghritaachi and others to disturb his concentration. But no matter what seductive acts they performed to make him attracted towards them, Vishwaroop, maintained his equipoise without caring for them the least. At last, resignedly, they left back to heaven and apprised their Lord about the failure of their mission. Getting utterly frustrated Indra thoght of nothing else and straight away hurled his thunderbolt at Vishwaroopa. But even the thunderbolt couldn't make any dent upon Vishwaroopa's concentration. Then Indra in further desperation made his friend Takshak hack off Vishwaroopa's all the three heads with his sharp tongue. It was a most heinous act on the part of Indra and hence he was condemned by all. Apart from that, he had the stigma of slaying a brahman attached to his head.

When Twashta heard about Indra's this most heinous act, in order to avenge his son's cold-blooded murder, he prayed the fire-God to get a most brilliant son called Vrita[1]. On his father's advise he prayed Brahma very devotedly to get the boon of remaining unslayable by any object made of iron, wood or other material. He was not to be slayed by any wet or dry weapon either.

Meanwhile, Indra carrying the charge for murdering a brahman upon his head, asked the divine Guru Vrihaspati as to how he should atone for this crime. But the Guru said: "You can't escape the cousequence of this heinous act. You have caused the death of a brahman ascetic. You'll have to suffer for it for long."

Soon after acquiring all the powers by virtue of the boon that he had recieved from Brahma, Vrittrasura (since he was fighting against the Gods, Vritra began to be called an Asura) attacked on heavens and snatched away all the precious gems and other prized possession of his brother's slayer Indra. All the Gods panicked before him and fled in panic. They went to the Lords, Brahma, Shiv and Vishnu but none could offer them any protection against Vritrasura's onslaughts. Only Vishnu advised them to worship the Supreme Goddess. The Goddess, eventually pleased with their devotion, promised them help at due time.

Then Vishnu instructed Indra in a bit of diplomacy. He asked Indra to seek friendship through the mediation of the top sages since Vritra could he over powered only through the trick of friendship. "Befriend Vritra, with his confidence and then cause damage to him under the facade of friendship," was the advice given to Vritra by shriwd Vishnu. Indra followed it totally and used the good offence of the sages to befriend Vritra. Consequently, the two developed friendship and started living peacefully. Although seeing this drastic

---

1. According to Sanskrit grammer and terminology, 'Vri' means Indra and 'Tra' means the destroyer. Hence Vritra means destroyer of Indra.

change in Indra's strategy, Twashta was apprehensive, and even warned his son about Indra's intentions, yet the Great Goddess's influence made Vritra indifferent to this warning.

One day when Indra and Vritra were wandering on the shores of the ocean at the pictursque dusk time, Indra thought his moment had come. He covered his thunderbolt with the foam gathered on the collection of the waves which was neither wet or dry. This way he fulfilled the condition necessary to make his weapon effective on Vritra. He hurled it at Vritra, chanting eventually the name of the Great Goddess. The weapon slayed Vritra in no time. Although Indra managed to get rid of his potential enemy in Vritra, yet he had again committed a deadly sin. Killing yet another brahman. With the result, he was again forced to roam around here and there and couldn't get his divine throne by the ruling of the divine order.

Nahush's Fall

Meanwhile, seeing the divine throne vacant, the divinities were scared, lest some other mortal should try to grab it. In order to avoid this eventuality, they asked the ruler of the earth, Nahush to occupy it. Nahush was delighted. He not only occupied the divine throne but also desired to have physical union with Indra's wife Shachi. As the morality-code of the divine world was, whosoever occupied the divine throne had, ex-officio, right to enjoy the women of the previous Indra. Although at the complaint of Shachi, Vrihaspati tried to dissuade Nahush from desiring copulation with Shachi, Nahush snubbed the divine Guru by saying: "Since when this rule has become effective in divine realm? Didn't Moon have physical relations with your wife Tara? Moreover, when Indra himself deceitfully enjoyed physical pleasure with the sage Gautam's wife Ahilya, why didn't the divine Guru invoke this rulling. Why is it reserved only for the mortal man? Sorry, I can't heed to your advice!"

When Vrihaspati failed to deter Nahush, Shachi was greatly nervous. Vrihaspati again advised her to seek the shelter in the Supreme Goddess's shelter. Shachi did so and the Goddess blessed her that not only her honour would he saved she would also get back her lost husband."

Getting this boon, Shachi was happy but to get rid of Nahush's advances she communicated the message to him: "I'm now going on a journey to the holy spots. I would bow before your desire when I return." Nahush agreed to wait.

While roaming about the earth's holy spots she happened to meet Indra passing his days of exile hidden in a huge stem of Lotus deep with in the ocean. Learning from Shachi about Nahush's lecherous desire Indra advised her. "That Nahush is now arrogant having grabbed the divine throne. You ask him to come to your palace carried in a palanquin loaded on the shoulders of the Seven Sages. If Nahush accepts this condition, he is sure to be thrown back to earth." As Shachi returned to the divine realm she sent this very message to Nahush. He readily agreed, drunk as he was in the wine of arrogance. As he was being carried in a palanquin by the Seven Sages, he repeatedly asked them to move fast, saying "Sarp-- Sarp[1]" Where upon, enraged by Nahush's temerity, Sage Agastya cursed him." Since you repeatedly utter 'Sarp--Sarp', you better become a serpent and return to earth in that very form." Immediately Nahush became a serpent and was thrown back to the earth. Concluding the story Sage Vyas told Janmejaya: "O scion of the Pandava dynasty! One should never be arrogant no matter what be one's achievements. In fact arrogance is the greatest enemy of the noble persons."

Janmejaya said. "Indeed it is, Sir! Just, greed and arrogance cloud one's discretionary vision. See the example of Indra only. In order to ensure his selfish intrest he didn't mind committing the most heinous act. Another one is of Nahush whose arrogance caused his down-fall from such lofty heights."

Vyas Ji says: "In fact the whole world pulsates with the inkling of the Supreme Goddess. She makes the entire universe exist in which only that happens which She wills. All the Gods including Vishnu, Brahma and Mahesh act at her behest only. Hence it is foolishness to be arrogant at one's individual achievement or greedy to ensure

---

1. In Vedic Sanskrit 'Sarp' means 'to move fast'. Perhaps, since the snakes more very fast, they came to be called 'Sarp'.

pleasures eternally. It is the Goddess's will that rules the roost here. Neverthless, trapped in it were even the great sage like Vashishtha and Vishwamitra." Then on Janmejaya's request the sage began narration of the episode involving a feud between Vashishtha and Vishwamitra.

Vashishtha And Vishwamitra's confrontation

Raja Harishchandra was the ruler of Ayodhya and a bright scion of the Solar Dynasty. When he didn't get a son for long he requested his family priest Vashishtha to guide him so that he might get a son. The sage advised Harishchandra to worship Varuna. Varuna, after a devout worship, was duly propitiated and he agreed to give a son to the king provided the latter returned him after performing a massive Yagya. The King, Harishchandra agreed. He duly got a son and when the son was grown up he also performed a massive Yagya. But he developed great affection for his son and refused to give him back to Varuna. This breach of promise made Varuna curse Harishchandra that he might be afflicted with dropsy. However, when the son of Harishchandra learned about the cause of his father's deadly illness, he offered to sacrifice his life at the altar of the Yagya. But Harishchandra never agreed to it. Then Vashishtha advised him.

"O King! In case you don't fulfil the condition you will suffer the disease. However there is one way out. You sacrifice some other lad in place of your son. This shall considerably initigate the felony." Wherupon Harishchandra gave a lot of wealth to a person called Ajigarta, and bought his son. But as that boy reached near the altar of sacrifice he started crying. Vishwamitra was also present there and he requested the King to be kind to that boy. But Harishchandra refused. This made Vishwamitra quite angry and seizing his opportunity be kidnapped the king. When Vashishtha learnt about it, he cursed the sage Vishwamitra to become a heron. This made Vashishtha also counter the curse by saying: "You become a crane." Although the issue was not that big yet the two big sages clashed due to their reckless ego. Eventually they both suffered the respective curses and at due time Brahma affected a patch-up between them.

Telling this the Sage Vyas said: "So, Janmejaya, you see that no matter how learned one be the streak of indomitable arrogance can make all commit even the most silly act."

Then narrating the episode to highlight how even the noblest brahmans due to adverse circumstances could be forced to act lowly, the sage Vyas started another story.

Once the king called Nimi appointed Vashishtha to perform a massive Yagya but the latter was committed to perform a ritual worship in the divine realm at Indra's invitation. But Nimi thought that Vashishtha was postponing his Yagya due to his (Vashishtha) greed for getting better reward from the divine worship. So he decided to have the ceremony performed under the priesthood of the sage called Gautam.

When Vashishtha returned from heaven he found that Nimi had already performed the Yagya. Feeling insulted Vashishtha cursed Nimi that he would have to lose his body. Nimi, feeling hurt due to the sage cursing him out of his sheer greed hurled a counter-curse at Vashishtha that he would also be losing his body soon. Eventually Vashishtha left that frame to get another birth through the womb of Urvashi with the seed of Mitravaruna, while Nimi refused to get another body and accepted to remain in the eye-lids of the descendant of his Videha dynasty.

Commenting upon the episode Vyas Ji said: "O King! both Nimi and Vashishtha were at fault. There was, in fact, hardly any big reason to make the king curse his family priest and the priest to curse his king. But it is really the evil sentiments like, greed and ego, that made them act that way." Continuing the narration to highlight the influence of ego-instincts that caused the nobles down-fall, the sage said: "Even the descendants of the great sage Bhrigu suffered their doom because of greed." Then he told another story.

The Tale of Haihaya Dynasty

Once the descendants of the Haihaya dynasty doled out a huge wealth to those staying in their Gurukul [School run by their Guru]. But as their bad luck would have it, after some time the descendants of that dynasty fell on evil days. They demanded financial help from those brahmans who became rich by their doling out the wealth. But all the brahmans said that they had no money And in order to secure their wealth the brahmans quietly buried it underground. But the Haihaya Kshatriya learnt about it. Enraged at their stinginess the Kshatriyas began to torture the brahmans; they didn't spare the brahmans' womenfolk. Distressed the brahmans scattered and fled elsewhere to survive. At last their women, on the advice of a sage started worshipping the Great Goddess. Duly propitiated the Goddess appeared before them and blessed: "My temple would be a safe haven for you. Built one and stay there." So they did. When the Kshatriyas again attacked the brahmans, the latter became blind due to the Goddess's influence. At last resignedly the Haihaya descendants left and the brahmans lived happily there.

Commenting upon this episode the sage, Vyas told Janmejaya: "O Descendent of an exalted Kshastriya dynasty, eschew greed for it causes the fall of the noblest. All material possessions are fey and transistory. The permanent wealth in this world is only the worship of the Great Goddess. Remain devoted to her and no damage can touch you."

Whereupon Janmejaya desired to know in details about the Haihaya dynasty of the Kshatriyas. "How come that they became as much poor as to be compelled to eye the wealth they had themselves doled out?"

Then Vyas Ji told him about them. Once in the realm of Vishnu, Vaikuntha, there arrived the sage Rewat, astride on the divine steed, Uchchreishrava. The horse was so beautiful that Lakshmi felt entraced by its beauty and consequently became indifferent to Vishnu and the sage dispite Vishnu's hidding her to properly welcome the sage Rewat. Angry at his espouse's indifference Vishnu cursed Lakshmi: "Henceforth you shall ever remain fickle and shall keep on roaming about the earth."

When Lakshmi became conscious of the curse, she requested her Lord to modify it as she really didn't want to insult the sage or be indifferent to Vishnu. Then Vishnu said: "All right. You will have to roam about the earth but in the form of a mare. After producing a son in that form you will regain your position and status."

Consequently Lakshmi came on to the earth in a mare's form and reaching the confluence of the river Tamasa and Yamuna began to worship Lord Shiv. Appearing before her the Lord said: O Devi! There is no difference between me and Lord Vishnu basically we are the same since we derive strength from just one source the Primal Goddess! "Lakshmi recollected that this secret was once revealed by Lord Vishnu as well. Then Lord Shiv asked her to have her desired boon. Lakshmi told him all about the curse she had received from Vishnu and desired redemption from it "Don't worry, Lord Vishnu would himself appear as a horse before you. Then he would create a son for you out of the physical union. As you do so, your curse period would end!"

Eventually when the appointed time came Vishnu appeared on the earth in the form of a horse and and having produced a son with his union with Lakshmi in the form of the mare, returned with Lakshmi back to heaven. Vishnu had entrusted that son's custody to the sage Turvasu for looking after him. This boy was called Haihaya. Later on he became a powerful king. He was the founder of the Haihaya dynasty.

At the conclusion of the story, Janmejaya further asked: "O Sage! Please also tell me the cause of the Haihaya's descendants becoming so poor that they had to request financial help from their own preist." Whereupon the Sage Vyas told Janmejaya the following story.

Once a powerful king of this dynasty (Haihaya), named Ekaveera saw a girl weeping in a lonely jungle where he had gone for hunting. That girl was the friend of the daughter of the another king Rainya. Both the friends had gone to collect flowers to the Jungle for worship. That girl's name was Yashomati and that of the princess Ekavali. In that Jungle a demon named Kalketu abducted Ekavali. Although Yashomati requested the demon to let go of the princess and have her in exchange, the demon refused. He was waiting to have physical union only with that princess and he even sought help of Yashomati to make Ekavali agree for having the physical union. Yashomati couldn't have done it. But desperately she started crying for help. The king Ekaveera thought it to be his moral duty to help Ekavali. He left for the search of that distressed princess. Soon he found that princess lying tied which demon Kalketu was also nearby, using a 'Beeja-Mantra' to have sex-with in that princess. When the king Ekaveera told him that it was wrong to forcibly copulate with an unwilling girl, the demon refused to listen to him. Whereupon the king hurled his weapon upon the demon. Though he died but since his Beeja-Mantra had become effective, his subsequent curse proved quite efficacious. The demon had cursed the king Ekaveera that his whole clan would become very poor once. Hence the Hai haya dynasty's descendant had to suffer poverty.

Having heard this story Janmejaya again asked: "O Sage! But I am surprised to know that even the sustainer of the world, Lord Vishnu had to face the curse and go down to the earth as a horse. Why? Kindly enlighten me."

Sage Vyas said: "O King! Remember that one can't escape the consequences of one's action no matter who he or she be. In fact his taking birth as a horse was the inevitable consequence of the curse that he charged Lakshmi with. The moment he said that Lakshmi would be redeemed from the curse of being a mare after producing a son, it was inevitable that son was to be sired by no one else but Vishnu since no one else could have physical union with Lord Vishnu's espouse."

Narada Becomes Monkey-Faced

In this context I may tell you what Narada Ji confided in me on my asking a similar question. I had asked Narada as to what was beyond any controversy and immutable. Then Narada Ji replied: "Sage! No one is beyond the reach of the divine illusion cast by the Great Goddess, whether it be Lords Vishnu, Brahma or Mahesh. Sage, I may tell you that even I was once trapped by it. Now listen to my experience." Then Narada Ji told the episode given below.

Once he and the Mountain-Lord Himavant went on to visit holy spots of the Aryavarta (undivided India). At the end of summers we happened to reach the capital of King Sanjaya. "We passed the four rainy months there only. The kind-hearted king asked his loving daughter to take special care of us. So, Princess Damayanti started to take care of our needs with a religious devotion. But she was mightly impressed by my lute playing. Hence she became rather extra devoted to me. The Mountain-Lord Himavant couldn't tolerate this discrimination and out of jealously he cursed me to became monkey-faced. I was taken aback by his temerity and I also cursed him to go and dwell on the earth."

"Although I became monkey-faced immediately, that princess continued to be devoted to me. But I felt very disappointed and forlorn at my ugliness. So I left living in the palace and started dwelling in a forest. But Damayanti came there as well. Since she was young and humble, her parents wanted to solemnise her marriage. They recieved many offers but Damayanti insisted on marrying me only. Although King Sanjaya tried his level best to dissuade her, she would stick to her guns. At last the king had no choice but to solemnise my marriage with Damayanti. We started living seperately. Once the Mountain-Lord Himavant happened to reach there again. Seeing him I bowed to him. Now he was also repentful and he withdraw his curse, leaving me again as I was."

Concluding the Sage Narad: "So Vyas Ji. At times even the learned persons like we also are carried away by our petty egoes."

Thus satisfying Janmejaya's query by this reference Sage Vyas said: "So, King, no body can say that he or she is beyond all weaknesses. One is free to act but once the act is committed no one can escape its consequencess. The world is full of pitfalls. Only those who carry the Supreme Goddess's image in their heart are able to skip them. She is the only refuge of all whether men, Gods or demons. She has no other alternative; nor there is any who could be equated with Her."

❑❑

Seventh Chapter.......

Janmejaya requested to Sage Vyas that since he had learnt about the extreme devotion to the Goddess of most of the kings of the Solar and the Lunar Dynasties (Surya and Chandravanshi rulers), he wanted to hear further about it from the sage's blessed mouth. Vyas Ji responded by telling about those kings in this manner.

Creation-Commenced

When born out of the Lotus protruding from Vishnu's navel, Brahma, devotedly hymned the glories of the Super Goddess she appeared before him and instructed him to start the process of creation. The first psychic issues of Brahma were Marichi, Angira, Atri, Vashishtha, Pulaha, Ritu and Pulastya. Then were born Daksha, Narad, Sanaka, Sanatan, Sanandan and Sanatkumar and a woman called Veerini who became Daksha's wife. Daksha first produced five thousand sons from Veerini and they were called Haryesva. When these sons were about to multiply the world through procreation, Narada happened to advise them that they should do only after they had measured the entire earth. But once they set out for this job they never returned.

Learning about Haryesva group vanishing, Daksha again produced another group called Shlashva who were again led astray by Narad. Third time Daksha produced 33 daughters. Thirteen out of them were given in marriage to sage Kashyapa from whom the sage produced entire creation of birds, reptiles, men, Gods etc. Hence the present creation is also called Kashyapa Creation.

Among the Gods there was one Vivasvawan whose son Manu is said to be the origin of all human beings. Manu had nine sons:

Ikshvaaku, Naabhag, Dhrishta, Sharyeti, Narisyant, Pranshu, Nrisha, Dishta, Karush and Prishadha. Among these Ikshvaaku was most brilliant who achieved many laurels to enhance the prestige of the Solar dynasty. Nabhag's son Ambareesha was also a brilliant and famous ruler. From Dhrishata were produced the clan of Kshatriyas called Dhashtark. The world-remowned ruler, Ararta's was Sharyati's son. Sharyati's one daughter Sukanya was married to the most ugly sage Chyavana. It was her wifely fidelity which made the divine physicions Ashwins Kumars convert the ugly, old sage Chyavan into a handsome youth. In return Chyavan had made the duo drink nectar.

Janmejaya was curious to know in detail about this story of Sukanya and Vyas Ji narrated it this way.

Sukanya-Chyavan Story

Once King Sharyati happened to go for hunting with his queens and his only daughter Sukanya. They stayed near a beautiful pond. Close to that pond sage Chyavan was busy in meditation. He had been doing it so devotedly many years that his entire body had been covered by Deemaka (termite), leaving just two holes near his eyes uncovered. While roaming about there Sukanya, out of sheer curiosity, pierced into the two holes in that Deemaka-mound (Chyavan) a sturdy, pointed piece of wood. She was bewildered to find the stream of blood oozing out from one of the holes. Unknowingly she had pierced Chyavan's one eye. Writhing in agony the sage cursed that henceforth the entire visiting party including the King, his entourage queens and the daughter won't be able to bring out their body waste. This was surely a very painful curse. When the King enquired from his daughter, Sukanya, the reason for this curse she told about her mistake. Then the King requested the sage Chyavan to withdraw his curse but the sage put forth a condition: "You all could be normal only when you give your this beautiful daughter to me in marriage." But how could a beautiful young daughter have been married off to that literally moth-eaten, ugly and half-blind sage? The king refused. But Chyavana refused as well to compromise on his marriage proposal. At last the daughter realised that all were suffering because of her mistake. So she requested her father. "Sire! Please marry me to that sage. If I have committed this grave mistake it is only I who should suffer the consequences of it." Although the king didn't agree with his daughter's proposal yet seeing the condition of his entire party he relented. At last Sage Chyavan had Sukanya as his wife. Showing her exemplary wifely devotion she refused to have anything from the royal dowry and left to the woods with his husband, that ugly, half-blind, old Chyavan. Without caring for the ugliness of her husband she devotedly looked after the sage's all comforts Chyavan was delighted at having such a devoted and extremely beautiful wife.

Once when Sukanya went to take bath in the nearby pond, the divine physicians Ashwinikumars, were loitering there. They were captivated by Sukanya's charms and offered to grant them immortal youth only if she could have physical union with them. They further said: "You're not fit with that old and ugly sage and you deserve physical union with the handsome youth like we are." But condemning them Sukanya said: "I am happy and satisfied with my husband. If you say anything further about my husband and your obscence offer, I would cast a deadly curse on you."

The divine physicians were delighted to see such a staunch wifely fidelity of Sukanya. They took her to guide them to her busband and as a reward to her staunch loyalty to her husband, they made Chyavan handsome and young by their divine medicines. In return Chyavan promised that he would make them drink nectar despite the expected objection from the divine lord, Indra's side.

It was after some time that when Sharyati happened to visit his daughter he was surprised to find her daughter living with a very handsome youth. When he learnt that he was no one else but the old and ugly sage Chyavan, Shryati's joy knew no bounds. Then Chyavan requested the king to hold a massive Yagya so that he could make Ashwini Kumars drink nectar as promised.

Returning to his capital Sharyati held such is massive Yagya that all the Gods and other beings were invited to it, including Ashwini Kumars. At the conclusion of the ceremony when, alongwith other senior Gods, Chyavan also offered nectar to the divine physicians, Indra objected to their being worthy of that divine potion. But when

Chyavan refused to listen to Indra's advice, Indra hurled his thunderbolt at him which was easily evaded by the sage. Then Indra created a deadly device for slaying the sage. Whereupon, as the counter measure, Chyavan created a maddened demon called 'Madarakshasa' which tortured the divinities to no end. At last when Indra sought his Guru, Vrihaspati's advice, the mentor advised him to cease fighting against that most capable sage and seek truce with him. Resignedly Indra accepted the advice and Chyavan fulfilled his promise by treating Ashwini Kumars on nectar.

Continuing the detail of this dynasty further Vyas Ji told Janmejaya that Sharyati's son Anarta had a son called Revata who had hundred sons called Kukudam and one daughter named Revati. When the daughter became nubile Revata went all the way to Brahma's realm to get the creator's advice for choosing a bridegroom for her. But Brahma told him: "Revata! You have no idea about time-cycle in different realms. While here you have passed a few moments only, on the earth many centuries would have elapsed by now. Now you return to earth and give your daughter to Yaduvanshi Balrama (Lord Krishna's elder brother) as he is the ideal choice for your daughter." Returning to earth Revata did so. Meanwhile, in the absence of Revata the demons had troubled his sons as much as to make them seek safety in the hilly terraine of Kashmir.

The Ikshavaku Dynasty

While telling in details about Ikshvaku Vyas Ji told Janmejaya that he was a most powerful king of the Solar dynasty. He had 100 sons and the eldest one was Vikukshi. Once Ikshaku told Vikukshi to bring some fresh meat from the jungle. He went there and collected enough meat. Since he felt himself hungry he ate a rabbit's meat and gave the rest of the collected meat to his family priest, Vashishtha. When Vashishtha learnt from his Yogic power that a part of the collected meat had been eaten, he told the king Ikshaku about it. In anger Ikshvaku turned his son out of the kingdom.

However, after Ikshavaku's death Vikushi it was who ascended the throne with the name Shashad. His son Kukustha was renowned as Indravaha.

Once when the demons attacked the gods' realm they sought Vishnu's advice who sent them to Kukustha. Kukustha had received the boon from the Super Goddess of invincibility. So Indra made him the commander of the divine Army who accepted to lead on the condition of Indra acting as his vehicle. Though Indra hesitated initially, yet at Vishnu's advice accepted Kukushtha's condition. Since he rode upon Indra's shoulders he came to be known as Indravaha.

Then the dynasty progressed this way: Kukustha son was Aneta>Prithu>Chandra> Yuvanashva> Sharant> Vrihadashwa> Kukshlashwa> Dritashva> Hriyasva> Nipumb> Bahirkashwa> Kripashwa>Presenjit>Yuvanashwa whose son was Mandhata.

Mandhata Story

Telling about how Mandhata got this name Vyas Ji told Janmejaya that Mandhata was actually produced from the body of his father and not from his mother's womb. In fact it so happened that Yuvanashwa failed to recieve any male issue from his all the queens then on the sage's advice he decided to perform a huge Yagya to propitiate the deities so that he could get a son. Since Yuvanashwa felt very thirsty in the day long continuing Yagya while sitting before fire, in the night, by mistake be drank the concentrated water. When in the morning the sages learnt about this mistake they beat their heads in frustration. However, by that time the consecrated water had starting showing its effect and Yuvanashwa's body showed the symptoms of some thing developing inside it. Then the expert sages performed an operation and brought out the boy from Yuvrashwa's body. Due to the effect of the Mantra both father and son remained alive with no damage to their body.

However, the problem arose about feeding the child as a male body had no provision for it. So in reply to this query: "Who should feed it," Indra said: "Man+dhata" [I would provide him nourishment]. Hence the boy came to be known as Mandhata.

Vashishtha And Vaishwamitra's Second Feud

Mandhata was married to Bindumati, the daughter of King Shashibindu. This union produced two brilliant sons: Purukutsa and

Muchukunda. Purukutsa had Aranya as son who produced Vrihadashwa. His son was Hriyashva whose son was Tridhanwa who produced Aruna. Aruna's son was Satyavrata who was lecherous by nature. Once he fell for a brahman girl and snatched her from the holy altar just before her marriarge.

Whereupon, the grieving brahman complained to the king who condemned his son for his heinous act and eventually turned him out of the place to make him forcibly longuish among the pariahs. But the family preist Vashishtha remained a mute spectator to this entire incident without intervening in the least. Satyavrat was angry at Vashishta who should have told him as to how to atone for this sin of committing this outrage with a brahman's daughter.

It was, however, sheer coincidence that as Satyavrata was exiled from the kingdom the state was gripped by a terminable drought. At that time leaving his family back home, sage Vishwamitra had gone to do a special penance. Facing the drought his wife thought of selling her one son to save the life of the remaining children. When Satyavrata heard about the appalling indigence of the sage's family, he intervened at the right time to protect the sage's son from being sold. Not only that he decided to look after all needs of sage Vishwamitra's family till his return. Every day he would kill beasts and send their meal to the sage's family for its bare survival. Once while searching for a prey he happened to spot sage Vashishtha's cow. Since he was already angry with Vashishtha, in sheer vegeance he took the cow in his possession, killed it and had its meat sent to sage Vishwamitra's family. Meanwhile Vashishtha learnt about his this abominable act and he cursed Satyavrata to become a real pariah. Owing to suffering his father's anger, kidnapping a brahman's daughter and facing the Guru's wrath, Satyavrata also come to be known as Trishanku. Feeling quite forlorn he decided to commit suicide while chanting Super Goddess's name. The Goddess was soon propitiated by his worship and blessed him that in no time he would be escorted back to his father with full honours and that he would be duly annointed as the king. Believing the Goddess's boon he began to wait for the materialisation of the Goddess's prediction.

Meanwhile, Narad reached near his father and apprised him of Satyavrata's deeply felt mortification, remorse and his ensuing repentence. Listening it father's natural affection for his son did well up. He ordered his commander to honourably bring Satyavrata, making the Goddess prediction come true. As Satyavrata returned to the kingdom he was formally asked to atone for his sins. Then he was duly made the heir apparent. But as his father retired to the forest completing his term as the king, the people, owing to their mind-washing done by Vashishtha out of the old grudge against Satyavrata, continued to call him a pariah. At last, in frustration he bequeather his throne to his son Harishchandra and finally left for the jungle, never to return.

But now Vishwamitra had come back from his penance and learnt all about Satyavrata's helping his family in the most distressing time. Vishwamitra was touched by Satyavrata's noble act and by his Yogic power he made Satyavrata ascend to the heaven while still being in his mortal body.

But Indra, knowing about the details and calling Satyavrata a pariah, sent him back to the earth. Beholding Indra's impudence to flout his command, Vishwamitra then decided to create a seperate heaven. When Indra learnt about this firm decision of the sage Vishwamitra, he took back Satyavrata but placed him between the heaven and the earth. Hence Trishanku means one who is left hanging between two realms.

Satyavrata's son Harishchandra had no male issue. When he worshipped Varuna, he got a son out of Varuna's grace [As has already been told earlier] He refused to part with his that so and give him back to Varuna after the promised Yagya, Instead he decided to offer the sacrifice of a bought son of a poor-man Ajigarta Shunashepa. Although this way Harishchandra satisfied Varuna by fulfilling his promise yet in the process he angered Vishwamitra by not releasing Shunashepa. Owing to this reason he had to suffer sage Vishwamitra deadly wrath.

☐☐

Eighth Chapter.......

Veridicious Harishchandra's Story

Janmejaya then, requested Sage Vyas to relate to him the story about the most veridicious king of all times, Satyawadi Harishchandra. VyasJi said: "Once in the court of Harishchandra, sage Vishwamitra arrived. Later on, when relaxing in the Solar family's priest Vashishtha's hermitage Vashishtha praised his king for the latter's truthfulness and noble character. But Vishwamitra objected. 'Don't forget how he sacrificed Shuneshepa in the place of his son dispite that poor boy's pathetic pleading. Even when I asked your king to be a bit kind hearted and release that poor lad, he had cared nothing before his selfish interests. In fact his entire show of veridiciousness and a truthful, noble conduct is nothing but a sham. Give me time, I will prove that he is a man of mean conduct." Giving this challange Vishwamitra departed in a huff and started waiting for the opportune moment to prove his charge on Harishchandra.

Once while hunting in the forest King Harishchandra saw a girl crying. On being asked she told that though everthing was fair and just in his kingdom, yet she was distressed on account of the adament and old sage Vishwamitra trying to possess her. She requested him to provide relief from Vishwamitra's demand. Thinking with compassion, Harishchandra made Vishwamitra stop in his penance to get that girl. But the king's interupting the penance of the sage as though added fuel to the fire of vengence already burning in that sage's heart. He by his mysterious powers connived with a demon who adopting the form of a deadly wild bear began to disturb all the people of the king's kingdom. At last on the people's request the king himself decided to kill that bear. While searching for that wild beast the king happened to reach the bank of a river where he found a brahman who was no one else but Vishwamitra himself in disguise. When the king asked him the way to Ayodhya, the brahman told him the way but advised the king that since that river granted great religious merit to the bather, he might as well take a dip in it. The king did so. Then after worship the religious minded king asked that brahman to recieve elms from himself as was customary. Whereupon the brahman a said: "O King! I want nothing for myself but I have to solemnise my son's marriage. Can I come at the due time to get elms from you." Assuring him that he could do so any time the king returned to his capital.

In a few day's time that brahman reached there. He was actually Vishwamitra in disguise. When he reminded the king of his promise, the king asked him to get anything as elms from him. The brahman then, demanded his entire kingdom. Bound by his promise the king readily agreed. Then the brahman said: "You have also to give me Dakshina (a kind of fees for completing the religious ritual on behalf of the host) which is two mounds of gold. Now how would you give it since your entire kingdom is mine" Bewildered, the king begged two months grace time to settle the account and left with his wife and son, Rohitashwa. Since Raja Harishchandra's rule stretched to entire earth which the king had donated to that brahman, he couldn't have gone anywhere save Kashi, reckoned to be a place beyond the world.

But arranging two mounds of gold was not easy. His wife decided to help him in a daily job which fetched them a few pice. However, the brahman didn't let Harishchandra get rid of him and presented himself in Kashi as well to remind about the due gold that the king had still to give. Feeling quite desperate, the king then decided to sell off his wife along with his only son. Though he got some money but it was still not enough. With the result he had to seek employment at a crematorium. He was appointed the Chaukidar (guard) there by the one who managed the crematorium.

Meanwhile, during the course of playing with a ball at the house of the man who bought Harishchandra's wife, Rohitashva was bitten by a snake and he cried. But the owner of the house didn't let

Rohitashva's mother leave the day's work unfinished. So at night when she went near her son, she found him dead-crying bitterly she took her son's body for cremation to that very crematorium where Harishchandra was employed. He couldn't recognise his wife and demanded due money for cremating the son. Then seeing the dead son's face he recognised him as well his wife and started weeping bitterly. He adviced his wife to worship 'Shatakshee Goddess' since in that terrible condition only she could provide them relief. As his wife did so, with the grace of the Super Goddess not only Indra and other Gods appeared praising Harishchandra's incomparable honesty but they asked Indra also revive the son back to life. At that time Vishwamitra also reached there, praising Harishchandra a loud. "Never has the world seen such an honest and truthful person. I admit that I was wrong and Vashishtha was right. I give your entire kingdom back to you and release you from all the debts that you owed to me." Harishchandra was delighted and appointing his son as his successor he left with his wife for the heaven, acompanied by the Gods.

Concluding the legend Vyas Ji said: "Janmejaya! It was the Goddess Shatakshee that shed her grace upon that beleagured king to end his all troubles."

Janmejaya queried: "O Sage! I am thrilled to know about such an honest king. But Sir, tell me, who is this 'Shattakshee Devi?"

Sage Vyas replied: "She is no other but Jagdamba the Great Goddess, mother of the Universe who had to assume once this form to kill a demon." Then he told Janmejaya the full story about the Great Goddess's appearing in this form.

Ruru's Tale

Once the descendant of the tyrant demon Hiranyaksha, Ruru, ruled over the demons realm. He soon relised that the source of all the Gods strength were the holy Vedas. Hence he decided to control the Vedas. With this intention he worshipped Brahma very devoutly. At last Brhma appeared before Ruru and granted him the desired boon. As he got control over the Vedas and hid them in the deep caves anarchy started to inflect every realm. All systems and rules went topsy turvy. Instead of remaining beyond the effect of time, the

Gods had started to aged, let alone the human and other species which lost all control of the righteous order. There was drought every where with all rivers and oceans drying up. At last the Gods and all beings prayed for relief from the Great Goddess. She appeared with hundred eyes on her face. She instantly killed that demon and restored the rightous order. Since she had a 100 eyes she came to be known Shatakshee. She promised all that a genuine prayer to her in the event of one's acute distress would have instant relief from her. With this promise she departed continuing to enlighten Janmejaya. Sage Vyas said: "It is the same Goddess who got different names on account of her adopting the needed form to rid the world of the evil. When the Gods found no vegetation on earth, she adopted the Shakambharee form to remove their distress; When she killed a demon called Durg she came to be known as Durga. But in reality it is one Primal Energy who is the Mother of all Universe and repository of all power in the world."

Janmejaya then asked: "Sage! Do the other Goddess like Lakshmi, Gauri (Parvati) derive their power from Her or they are the different forms of Her only?"

Vyas Ji said, "They are Her only but only in parts. Once these three Gods also developed some arrogance on account of the powers they commanded. It was again Her, the Great Goddess who put them back to their due position. I will tell in details about this episode."

The Super Gods' Arrogance

Once Shiv and Vishnu fought very long battles against the demons and managed to defeat them with the help of their spouses. But, eventually they won the battle and hence tried to express their superiority before their spouses. This made them laugh with derision. Feeling hurt the two Gods began to treat their spouses also with contempt. Whereupon the goddess left the Gods and disappeared, making the Gods quite lustreless and enervated. When Brahma saw this condition of his two top colleagues he decided to invoke the Great Goddess along with his all sons. The Great Goddess duly appeared before the Creator and on his request restored Vishnu and Shiv to their exalted status. But she warned them that they should never look down upon their female counterparts, else they might lose their real puissance. Since Daksha had played a big role in Her invocation, She blessed him that at due time She herself would come as his daughter, Sati.

Then Vyas Ji told him about Sati's tale and her eventually consuming herself in the holy pit of the Yagya performed by her father. However, she was again born as Gauri in the Mountain Lord Himavant's house. Meanwhile for killing the demon Tarak it become essential that Shiv should remarry to produce a son since Tarak was to be slayed only by Shiv's son. But, Shiv, having lost Sati, had become totally indifferent to have another wife. Though Kama-deva tried hard to arouse amorous feeling, in the process he lost his body. At last Shiv agreed to marry again. At due time he married Parvati and his son from that union slayed Tarak [This is a well known legend repeated already and hence has been given as a brief summary].

Shiv had actually agreed to marry second time when the Gods prayed to Super Goddess by Chanting the following Shloka:

NAMAH PRANAT ROOPAYEI
NAMO HEENKAR MOORTAYE
NATA MANTRATMIKAYEI
TEY KARUNAYEI NAMO NAMAH!

Thus propitiated Goddess assured the Gods that Shiv would surely marry Her mortal counterpart Gauri.

Concluding the story Vyas Ji said that "In a similar way, as the Super Goddess's bidding Vishnu was associated with the ocean's daughter Lakshmi ultimately it is the Great Goddess that is manifest everywhere."

Janmejaya again asked: "O Sage! Please tell me about Great Goddess's various forms and the places where each form is adored in a special way." Vyas Ji said: "This question was also once asked by Narada to Narayana I learnt this secret from Narad only. This is what he confided in me."

When Brahma asked his psychic son, Swayambhoo Manu to start creation of the world, Manu first worshipped the Great Goddess.

Manu had two sons. Priyavrata and Uttanapad and three daughters Aakooti, Devhooti and Prasooti. The daughters were respectively married to Ruchi, Kardam and Daksha. Devahooti produced Kapil, Aakooti Yagya and Prasooti many daughters. Manu's eldest son Priyavrata was married to Vishwakarma's daughter, Bahirishmati who was extremely beautiful. Once Priyavrata found one part of the earth to be perennially dark and the other bright. But he never wanted any part to remain dark in his empire. So, for diffusing the darkness, riding upon his chariot he came back to his palace and sharpened the wheels of his chariot. Then he travelled all over the earth to divide it in seven continents called the Jambudweep, Padmadweep, Shalamalidweep, Kushdweep, Kraunchdweep, Shkadweep and Pushkardweep. The measurements of these continents increased progressively, doubling every time. These were covered by Kshar, Ikshu, Sura, Ghrita, Dugdha, Dadhi, Takra and pure water oceans[1] respectively. Priyavrata divided his empire into these seven parts and made his seven sons rule each of them.

The Jambudweep And Its Sub-divisions

Telling in details about the Jambudweep, sage Vyas said that it spread to a hundred thousand Yojans[2] and looked round in appearance. The dwellers here worshipped Jagdamba as Jambavadini, Kokilaakshee, Karuna, Kaampoojita, Kottoor Vigraha, Maya and Gabhastani forms. A sub-division of Jambudweep was also called Ilavritta where the Super Goddess was worshipped as Neelambana, Raudramukhee, Phalada, Varada, Madanonmaadini, Maupriya, Maanpoojita and Meenalochana. In this part the water of the rivers was especially salubrious. Here the river Ganga that issued from the footnails of Lord Vishnu appeares very enchanting. Ilavritta was the region which was kept reserved for the amorous plays of Lord Shankar and Uma where any male's entry was prohibited. Any male who happened to tresspass into this region was bound to be converted into a female.

In the Bhadrashwa region resided Bhadradwa and his descendants. Here Lord Vishnu was worshipped in the form of

---

1. These Oceans were in other words filled with alkali, acid, wine, ghee, milk, curds, whey and pure water respectively.
2. Rughly equal to 2 miles=1 Yojan

Hayagreeva. In the region Ketumaal, Lord Narayan's brow-beater of Kama form, was worshipped along with the Ocean-born Lakshmi.

In the Ramyake region Lord Vishnu was worshipped in His Fish-In carnation form and Bhagwati Goddess in the female fish form. In the Hiranmaya region He (Lord Vishnu) attracted his devotees in the form of the tortoise Incarnation alongwith his espouse. In the north Kuru region Vishnu was adored in the Boar form while in Kimpurush region He was adored as Rama with the Wind-God's son Hanuman ever present in his chosen Lord Rama's service.

In Bharatavarsha the Four-Armed Vishnu and Goddess Mahamaya in her Eight Armed form were also worshipped. Here, there were many important mountain ranges like Malaya, Maniak, Sahri, Rishyamooka, Drona, Chitrakoot, Goverdhana, Raivatak, Neel and Kukum from which issued Tamraparnid, Kaverd, Tungabhadra, Godavari, Tapti, Rewa, Narmada, Sindhu, Saraswati, Yamuna, Gomati, Sarayu, Shatadru, Chandrabhaga, Vitastu etc. Here, according to the results of their past-life-deeds, the people were born dark, fair or semni-dark. However, owing to being the 'land of action' Bharatavarsha derived greater importance over other regions. Even the Gods longed to get birth in Bharatavarsha. The Jambudweep had eight subdivisions as informed before. The were Ilavritta, Bhadra, Ketumaal, Ramyaka, Hiranyamaya, morth Kuru, Kimpurush and Bharatvarsha.

The Description of Hells

Having discribed the various regions covered by the Jambudweep, Sage Vyas gave the following details about the hells situated amidst the earth and Patal-lok (the nether-realms), alongwith the crimes that took on to these hells.

    (i) **Tamisra** : He who steals other's women, property and issues goes to this hell. Here the being is so severely beaten by the messangers of the Death-Lord, Yama, that it may lose even his consciousness. The deadlier part of this hell is Andha-Tamisra to which a being is consigned when he rapes his patron or the mentor's wife. The tortures inflicted here blinds the being totally.

(ii) **Raurava :** He who gethers wealth through unfair means or through committing murder is consigned in here. In this hell the dangerous serpents keep on bitting the being. Those who indulge in murderous violence are consigned to Maharaurava which is the deadlier part of this hell. Here all the criminals meet their Nemesis.

(iii) **Kumbheepaak :** This is the hell for those who kill birds and animals and devour their flesh. Here the being is boiled in oil and tortured.

(iv) **Kaalsootra :** He who deceived brahmans and his elders goes to this hell. Here the being to starve perennially.

(v) **Asipatravana :** Those who deviate from the path ordained by the Vedas goes to this hell where the being are whipped and their body parts are hacked off with swords and knives.

(vi) **Sookaramukh :** The king who punishes an innocent brahman is consigned in this this hell. Where these arrogant tyrants are tortured till they become unconscious.

(vii) **Andhakoopa :** Those who torture the devotees of Gods are consigned to this hell where they are bitten by poisonous scorpions and other deadly insects.

(viii) **Krimibhojan :** He who devours the 'prasad' of a Yagya or other holy ceremonies is sent to this hell where he is forced to eat the food full of insects.

(ix) **Sadansha :** The smugglers and thieves who snatch other's money are consigned to this hell to get tortured by being stung by deadly and poisonous insects.

(x) **Tapta moorti :** The man or woman who establish physical contact with the persons of prohibitive category are consigned to this hell. Here they are forced to embrace the colomn made of red hot iron, and tortured in many ways.

(xi) **Shalmali Kantah :** Those who copulate with cheap women of easy virtue on the lure of some temptation are consigned to this hell.

(xii) **Vaiterani :** Those who maintain double standard for selfish, personal gains and support blesphemy are cousigned to this hell, full of hungry alligators who bite such persons to pieces.

(xiii) **Pooyoda :** The King who supports blesphemy and act shamelessly is consigned to this hell where he had to survive on a diet of dirty blood and pus.

(xiv) **Pranarodh :** The shameless lechers are consigned to this hell, full of urine and excreta. Where they suffocate for their entire term.

(xv) **Vishashan :** Those who employ blood-hounds or other ferocious dogs to kill harmless animals are sent to this hell where their body is continuously pierced by a pointed grass called 'Kusha'.

(xvi) **Lalabhaksha :** Those over sexed persons who force their espouse to indulge in oral sex are consigned to this hell where they are forced to drink semen only.

(xvii) **Saarmeyadana :** Those who buru villages and commit dacoity, loot others are consigned to this hell where blood-thirsty dogs eat away their physical self.

(xviii) **Aveechi :** Those who give false evidence deliberately and often forget about their resolution to donate elms to the needy are consigned to this hell where they are repeatedly dropped from mountain tops and thus tortured endlessly by forceing molten iron down their throat.

(xix) **Kshar Kardam :** Those who insult and shabbily treat the learned, erudite scholars and disobey their dictates are cousigned to this hell where they are placed head-long in the grime and filth.

(xx) **Rakshasbhoj :** Those who eat females flesh by killing them become themselves the food of those whose flesh they had consumed.

(xxi) **Shoolaprot :** Those who commit breach of trust and cause death to innocents are consigned to this hell where their gibbeted bodies are stung by deadly scorpions.

(xxii) **Dandashooka :** Those who unneccessarily torture the innocents and make them suffer agony are consigned to this hell where in a cave they are thrown before the many mouthed hungry deadly reptiles.

(xxiii) **Avata Nirodhana :** Those who imprison innocents in torture-chambers are consigned to this hell where they have to live amdist a most suffocating and obnoxious smoke.

(xxiv) **Jeeva Paryavartana :** Those who insult and shablily treat their invited guests are sent to this hell where they are paid back in the same coin.

(xxv) **Soochimukh :** Those who eye other's women or wealth and seize their opportunity to enjoy the same are consigned to this hell where their bodies are constantly peirced by sharp needles.

The Ritual Worship of the Goddess and Its Rewards

Vyas Ji said: "These details I gathered from a discussion between Lord Narayan and Narad Muni. Although there are many more hells these have been mentioned as an example to stress the fact that no crime is allowed to go unpunished. On the other hand, those who worship Super Goddess, repose faith in righteous order get equal number of heavens as well. In short, worshipping the Super Goddess is heaven and indifference to Her is hell."

Whereupon Narad wanted to know as to how the Goddess should be ritually worshipped. Answering him Lord Naryan said that although any time the Goddess could be worshipped with genuine faith with any material available for getting any desired result, however the scriptures have classified them in the following way. Nevertheless, for the Super Goddess the importance is of a guileless feeling and a genuine prayer.

The Chart For The Goddess's Ritual Worship

S.N.	Lunar Date	Material	The Material to be Donated	Rewards
1.	1st day	Flower garland	Ghee	Robust health.
2.	2nd day	Sugar	Sugar	Long age
3.	3rd day	Milk	Milk	End of sorrow
4.	4th day	Poori (loaf of ghee rich bread)	Poore	Removal of obstruction
5.	5th day	Banana	Banana	Enhanced wisdom

S.N.	Lunar Date	Material	The Material to be Donated	Rewards
6.	6th day	Honey	Honey, or other sweets	Beauty
7.	7th day	Jaggery product	Ladoos (of Jaggery)	Grief Overcome
8.	8th day	Coconut	Coconut	End of worries
9.	9th day	Beaten Rice	Beaten rice (Kheela)	Happiness
10.	10th day	Black Til	Black Til (sesame)	Life enhanced
11.	11th day	Curds	Butter (or Ghee)	Godess's grace
12.	12th day	Chewra or	Fresh rice corn	Goddess's happiness
13.	13th day	Grams	Grams (black)	Birth of a son
14.	14th day	Sattoo	Sattoo (roasted ground cereals added with sugar)	Lord Shiv's Grace
15.	Full Moon Day	Kheer	Kheer (rice cooked in rich milk with sugar)	End of affection.

The week-day schedule with material needed to gift away each day is the following:—

Monday-Milk; Tuesday-Banana; Wednesday-Butter; Thursday-Sugar; Friday-Khanda (Unrefined sugar); Saturday-Ghee made from cow's milk and Sunday-Kheer should be offered to the deity. According to the scriptures the Goddess's favourate eatables are Ghee, Til, Curds, Butter, Laddoo made from sugar, Banana, Coconut, Mausambi (a citrous fruit like orange) pomegranates, plums (per) and Kheer. One who worships the Goddess with true feelings she definetly answers one's prayer.

❏❏

NINTH CHAPTER.......

Continuing his narration, Soota Ji told the assembled sages that when Janmejaya heard about the ways of doing the ritual worship of the Goddess, he was delighted and said to sage Vyas: "O Sage! I am immensely grateful to you for your having enlightened me about the Goddess's ritual worship. Please also shed light on the various forms of the Goddess. Did she reveal herself suddenly? How had she appeared?" Sage Vyas answered: "O King! She is eternal like this earth, sky, time and space. In fact She is nature and the two should not and cannot be distinguished. How could you identify the Moon from the moon-grace, fire from heat and brilliance from light. It is she who creates the basic particles with which the whole world is created. She is not only the Srijankarta[1] but Sarjankarta[2] as well. It was She who happepned first of all and at Her inkling water, earth and sky were brought into eixstence. Then came Vishnu from whose navel was originated Brahma who created the rest of the creatures. Then appeared Shiv to dispose of the decadent and spent bits of creation. But these three Super Gods junction only at behest of the Goddess."

Outing the dialogue between Narayan and Narad Vyas Ji said: "Then Narayan said to Narad: "O Brahma! The Super Goddess revealed herself from her five partial creations from her left which are called Durga, Radha[3], Lakshmi, Saraswati and Savitri. From her right part were created Vishnu, Brahma and other male deities."

---

1. Creator who moulds different shape from the basic material already created.
2. Originator who first brings into the being the basic material.
3. Radha's is an eternal image who also incarnated in Dwaper Age to appear as a cow-maid girl when Krishna appeared as a cow-boy.

Then he told about Saraswati: "She is the Goddess of speech and all learning. She is also called Vak. The scriptures ordain that she should be worshipped on the fifth lunar day of the month of Magh in the bright fortnight. First the holy pitcher should be placed upon the concenrated spot. Then with all the 16 methods she should be ritually worshipped and as 'prasadam' fresh butter, Curds, honey, milk, til, laddoos, the juice of sugarcane, sweets, lentils, paste coconut, plum and banana should be offered, while Chanting the Mantra: "NAMO DEIVYEI SARASWATEI"

for eight times in one go.

This Beej Mantra was given by me to Valmiki, Who passed it on to sage Bhrigu who gave it to Shukracharya. From where this Mantra was received by Mareech who gave it to Vrihaspati. Yagyavalkya received it from him and this way this became popular." Vyas Ji said: "The scriptures say that one who chants this Mantra for for 4 lakh times, becomes so powerful that whatever desire he utters get's surely accomplished."

After the completion of the worship the following Shloka should be reverentially Chanted.
KRIPA KURU JAGANMATAH MAM EWAM HATTEJASAM
GYANAM DEHI SMRITI VIDYANI SHAKTI DEHI MANASWANI

Vyas Ji then told Janmejaya that once Janmejaya had totally lost his knowledge due to his Guru's curse. Then the Sun God advices him to worship Saraswati whose grace made him again fully learned.

Fight Between Ganga and Saraswati

"In fact Saraswati is the Goddess of heaven." Vyas Ji continued: "It is due to her having a quarrel with Ganga that she was forced to come down to the earth. When Narad Ji wanted to know the reason of their quarrel, Narayana disclosed this legend." Then Vyas Ji explained.

As a matter of fact, all the three Devis: Ganga, Lakshmi and Saraswati were dear consorts of Lord Vishnu. Once Saraswati developed grouse seeing Ganga having amorous love play with the Lord. She was very much disturbed and asked the Lord when she next met him: "O Master! Is it meet for you to show extra affection to your one consort while the other two long for your company? In that case you should have not chosen us. After all we are your consorts and have every right to be close to you?'

The Lord was quite perturbed seeing the dispute developing between Ganga and Saraswati. Although he had tried to be impartial yet when he found the two unrelenting, he left Vaikuntha in disgust. Seeing the Lord going out, Saraswati decided to settle her score with Ganga once for all. She grabbed Ganga by the latter's flowing hair. When Lakshmi tried to pacify both by espacially asking Saraswati to behave, the latter thought her to be siding with Ganga. Enraged, Sawaswati cursed Lakshmi that she would have to live on earth in the form of a tree. Ganga was also angry at the impudence of Saraswati and cursed the latter that she would have to remain on earth in the form of a river. In retaliation, Saraswati also cursed Ganga that she would have to descend not only on to earth but she would have also to carry all type of filth and grime alongwith the bones and tendons of the dead bodies.

When Vishnu came back and learnt about how the three goddess had cursed each other he said to them: "Now you shouldn't be sorry for what has already happened. In fact your cursing each other was caused by Providence. This was bound to happen. But you should not grieve for it, for, going down to earth each of you shall earn more renown. Henceforth Ganga shall be flowing mainly on the earth and only in token form she would remain near me. So shall be the fate of Saraswati. But, since Saraswati had tried to physically harras Ganga, she would go down first and would be flowing in the form of a river visible and invisible both. And Ganga would score more merit on earth than Saraswati. As for Lakshmi, she would be going to the earth in the form of the 'Tulsi' tree which I hold as the dearest. There she would also earn my love when I incarnate myself and shall be my wife on the earth as well."

Concluding the story, Vyas Ji said: "Since then Saraswati flows like a river on earth. Since the master of all ponds and streams water is called Saraswan, owing to they being her main source of water, she came to be known as Saraswati, or in other words the spouse of Saraswan."

Radha And Ganga

Vyas Ji then quoted a reference about the discussion between Sage Narad and Narayana. The query that Narad raised was that Ganga's name was not mentioned among the five manifest forms of the Super Goddess. So was she the same Ganga as referred to in the above story or was she a different existence? How she came to become so beloved of Lord Vishnu as much as to be called his espouse?

Then Narayan explained. "Radha is the presiding deity of the waters of Ganga. Once Radha-Krishna were so deeply engrossed in the 'Raas-Dance' that they were lost in the water flowing closely. Seeing Lord Krishna and Devi Radha disappeared, the Gods grew panicky. Then a voice arose from that water: "How are you all concerned with our physical form? Now behold our united form through this water-course now called Ganga."

Although Krishna also explained Radha the significance of that water called Ganga, she refused to believe. In order to test whether she was actually those waters' presiding deity, Radha drank up the entire water. The everessence of that rare and divine water perturbed the Gods. But in order to save her existence from her presiding deity's vengence, Ganga quickly entered a part of it, before it was drunk up by Radha, into the toe tail of Lord Krishna. A part of it filled the Kamandal (water-pot) of Brahma. Then she was again fully manifest when Vishnu as Vamana Avataar decided to measure the entire realm by his three footsteps and in the process when the second step measured the heavens Brahma reverentially washed it there and Ganga issued forth as the perennial stream. When it was brought down by Bhagirath's entreaties, a part of it remained confined to the divine river staying close to Vishnu. Since she carried Saraswati's curse, she had to come down to earth and flow as a perennial stream. "Owing to this fact it represented the joint form of both Radha and Krishna, The river is ever held to be the most sacrosanct water sources over all the realms."

Then Narad asked Narayana to narrate the story of Tulsi's association with Lord Krishna and he told this story.

Tulsi-Shankhchooda Story

Kushadhwaja was a powerful king in the older times. He was a direct descendant of Daksha. Kushadhwaj did so vigorous penance to please the Goddess of prosperity, Lakshmi, that she accepted to be born as his daughter. As she was born she was able to chant even the Vedic Mantra. That girl was named Vedavati. When she grew up he performed a vigorous penance to get a boon that she would get Vishnu as her bridegroom.

Once when she was busy in her penance, Ravan the demon-Lord appeared at her hut but in the form of a guest. Following the jungle tradition she welcomed him with fruits and other herbal eatables. But Ravan developed lecherous intentions seeing Vedavati's enchanting beauty. When the demon Lord tried to forcibly overpower her, blowing in rage she cursed him that it is on account of only a woman that he would eventually be distroyed. Then she burnt herself to death. It was she who was born in her future life as Sita, the espouse of Rama. However, in her next life she was born as a daughter to King Dharmadhwaj and queen Madhavi. This time her name was Tulsi. In order to get her desired boon she began to perform a vigorous penance. Brahma was eventually pleased with her and said: "O girl! You will marry a partial incarnation of Vishnu first and after some time you will get the real Vishnu."

As was ordained, at the appropriate time she was married to King Shankhchood who was Vishnu's partial form. He was quite a powerful King and soon he overpowered all the Gods, demons, Gandharvas and Kinnars. The defeated Gods reached near Brahma and Shiv who took then all to Vishnu's realm. Vishnu devised a plan and asked them to behave accordingly. As per the plan, Shiv despatched Pushpadant as the divine messanger to Shankhchooda for making peace. But Shankhchooda refused to listen to the divine plea. This forced Shankar to assemble the divine army including his pet henchpersons like Skand (his son), Veerabhadra and Bhadrakali and decided to attack Shankhchooda. Meanwhile, Shankhchooda told everything that happened there to his wife Tulsi and showed his fear for the inevitable war. But Tulsi asked him to forget about war and enjoy sensual bliss in her company.

In the morning the inevitable war commenced and Shakhchooda had to face the divine army led by Shankar. Although the war continued for about a 100 years it remained indecisive.

Meanwhile, according to his secret plan Vishnu reached before the king Chandrachooda and got from him the desired boon. The King granted it without knowing as to what he was allowing to that brahman.

In fact, the plan of Vishnu was to make Chandrachooda's wife Tulsi break her wifely fidelity vow since, till she maintained it, no one, not even any God could have even touched Chandrachooda.

So getting the desired boon, Vishnu adopted King Chandrachoods's form to such perfection as to confuse even his wife with his appearance. He had reached their announcing his victory over the Gods (as the King Chandrachood). The wife Tulsi accepted him as her husband and they passed the night together enjoying most amorous plays on bed. With the result, Tulsi's vow of infidelity was broken, leading to the real Chandrachood's certain defeat, since his source of power had vanished. Seeing him powerless Lord Shankar ended his life by his trident's blow.

But when Tulsi learnt about the trick Vishnu had played on her, she cursed him to get petrified as a stone. But Vishnu said "I did this all to fulfil your own wish-the one that she had expressed before Brahma long back: to get Vishnu as her husband." Hearing this Tulsi become as in inimate as a dead object and by Saraswati's curse became a tree (plant). And in conformily with the curse that Tulsi had cast upon him, he himself readily became a stone called Shaligram[1]. Then Brahma came there and got their eternal marriage completed.

Savitri's Story

Janmejaya then requested Vyas Ji to enlighten on Devi Savitri's character.

Vyas Ji said: "O King! The Goddess Savitri was first mainfest in Brahma's realm when the Creator with all Gods had worshipped her.

---

1. A pious stone believed to be Lord Vishnu's representation.

Subsequently, her one incarnation appeared on the earth as King Ashwapati's daughter.

Ashwapati was the King of the state called Madradesh. His wife and he remained issueless for many decades. So, they sought shelter in Vashishtha's advise, who advised the couple to worship Goddess Savitri. Getting these instructions they left their capital to reach Pushkar Kshetra. There they happened to meet sage Parashar who advised them to Chant non stop the holy Gayatri Mantra as its chanting while keeping face eastwards for 10 million times "would fulfil all your wants." One had to be very alert to count the exact number each time. "The best way," Sage Parashar said, "is to do so while moving your finger on the head or Rudraksha. Start this at a clean place." Then the sage enlightened the royal couple on its ritual." Choose the 14th day of the dark fortnight of the month of Jyeshtha (mid May to mid June). Place the holy pitcher on the consecrated spot. Invoke all the Gods. And then start the chanting. Complete this everyday with doling out elms, and continue till you have chanted the Gayatri Mantra a crore times."

Religiously following the sage Parashar's instructions, King Ashwapati and his wife did so and eventually they were blessed with Savitri's Darshan. The couple sought the boon: "Be you our daughter." "So be it," the Goddess said and disappeared.

Savitri & Satyavan

At due time Raja Ashwapati got a daughter. They called her 'Savitri' only. When she became nubile she was married off to Satyavan. But soon after the marriage Satyavan's father, a king, had lost his kingdom. The family with Savitri was forced to pass its days in exile in jungles. Once when Satyavan, on his father's instruction went to collect flowers for worship, he was bitten by a snake and he died. The death-God, Yamraj, took the soul of Satyavan and started moving to his realm. But to his great surprise he found Savitri' following him. Then she, on being questioned, replied him that a woman had no place to go in the absence of her husband. Then Yamraj told her about the rule of this ocean of worldly existence "where no one is any help to anyone and every one has to suffer the consequences of one's deeds." Whereupon Savitri countered the argument by saying that "I have heard that Mother Goddess's worship removes all the evil effects of one's past misdeeds," and eleborated on the metaphysical aspects of worship. Yamaraj was impressed by her erudite knowledge. He asked her to seek his desired boon. Savitri said: "this I was sure of since Darshan of the Deites never goes without the accompaying rewards. I want you to bless me that I may beget 100 sons." Yamaraj said: "So be it." But then the clever Savitri said: "Won't I be incurring infamy by begetting sons in the absence of my husband?"

Yamaraj found himself trapped since he couldn't have withdrawn his earlier boon to her. At last, he allowed a new lease of life for Satyavan and this way Savitri snatched back her husband from even the jaws of death.

Having herd this legend, Narad desired to know about the origin of Lakshmi. Narayana obliged him by telling him the following story.

Goddess Lakshmi's Origin

Once the divine chief, Indra, in an amorous mood was enjoying love-play with the Apsara, Rambha, when all of a sudden, the fiery sage, Durvasa, happened to pass through that lonely corner of the forest. Indra reverentially bowed to him. Pleased, the sage gave him the garland of Parijata flowers to Indra which the sage had recieved from heaven. But, without realising the worth of that rare garland, Indra casually placed it round the neck of his favourite mount, the elephant Eiravat. That pachyderm callously trampled that garland under its heavy feet. All this while Indra was enjoying his time with the Apsara. When Durvasa, with his Yogic sight, saw how that rare garland was contemptuously treated, he cursed Indra: "Now Goddess of all prosperity would leave you and you shall be a pauper. Realising his mistake Indra requested the sage to forgive him but that admant sage would not relent. At last Indra went to his mentor Vrihaspati who expressed his inability to help him and guided the divine chief to seek shelter under Vishnu's grace. Vishnu said that since Lakshmi had gone under water, deep in the oceans, only through massive churning of the ocean that she could be brought out. Then he advised

Indra that "alone you can't do it. You must seek all demons' help also." At last the sea was churned and Lakshmi came out. She immidiately chose Vishnu as her spouse[1]. As she came out, all the Gods led by Indra welcomed her back to existence. Then Indra Chanted the following Verse:

NAMAH KAMALVASINYEI NARAYANYE NAMO NAMAH.
KRISHNAPRIYAYEI SATATAM MAHALAKSHMI NAMO NAMAH.
AHAM YAVAT TYAYA HEENAH BANDHUHEENASHCH BHIKSHUKAH
SARVASAMPAT - VIHEENASHCHA TAVADEVA HARIPTIYA!

[O Great Goddess, the dweller on the lotus petal! Till I am devoid of you I am like a beggar estranged from friends, brothers and wealth. O Beloved of Hari! Only by getting your grace that I can get back, all my wealth, position and relations]

Praying thus, in extreme agony Indra started crying as well. Then the Goddess Lakshmi blessed him that she would never desert his realm.

Concluding the story, Narayan told Narada that all then were different, manifest form of the Super Goddess.

Then Narayan related to Narada the story of the origin of Durga and Radha (which have already been recounted) All these different forms should be worshipped by chanting the following Shloka.

NAMAH SARASWATI ROOPE NAMAH SAVITRI SHANKARI
GANGA DURGA SATI ROOPE NAMO LAKSHMI SWAROOPI NEI
MOOL-PRAKRITIROOPAN TWAN BHAJAMAH KARUNARNAVAAM
SANSARA SAAGARRAT ASMAN-UDDHAR-AMBA DAYAM KURU

[O Saraswati, Savitri, Shiva, Ganga, Durga, Sati and the Blessed forms of Lakshmi or Radhika-my repeated obeisance to you! O Goddess, ocean of compassion, in your prestine form-please redeem us; please incarnate on to this ocean of life and death, and have mercy on me].

Apart from this, **'NAMO BHAGVATYEI DURGA'** is also a consecrated Mantra.

---

1. The Sea-Churning legend is too well known to be recounted here. Hence its brief reference has been given here.

Manasa Devi

Getting this infornation about the different styles of worship of the Super Goddess, Narada said: "O Great Sage! Please tell me about the serpent Goddess Manasa also!"

Narayan said that she was also a manifested form of the Goddess Supreme. Telling about Manasa Devi, Narayana said: "Sage Kashyapa had been blessed with a daughter named Manaasa by the Super Goddess. When she came of age he was married to Jaratkaru. It was from this union that Asteeka was born who had played the major role in stopping the Yagya that Janmejaya had performed to cause the extinction of the serpents' species."

Continuing to relate to Narada the story Narayan said: "Since one of the abodes of the Super Goddess has also been the Mountain Vindhya, she is also called Vindhyavasini." Whereupon Narada asked Narayan about this famous mount Vindhya and how it once had stalked the progress of even the Sun. Then the great sage Narayan related to Narad the following legend.

Mount Vindhya's Anger

Once loitering all over the world, the divine sage Narad, an expert in confusing people, reached near the mount and started having long sigh's of anguish. When the Mount asked: "What is the cause of your unhappiness? What is disturbing your composure?"

Narada said: "O Great Mount! You know how impartial are we sages in our outlook. Any injustice done to one rankles in our conscience. I find the sun regularly perambulating round the Himalayas and Gandhamadan etc. but you stand neglected because of your less height."

This was enough to sting the arrogant mount to the quick. He started rising as much as to block even the sun's curse. With the result, half of the world continued to be plunged into darkness while the other half remained to be ever lighted. A massive imbalance was created in the global order. The Gods rushed to Lord Vishnu who said: "Vindhya could be held back from rising only by sage Agastya. He is now busy in his worship of the Great Goddess in Kashi." The

Gods then rushed to Kashi and with much attempts managed to make Agastya agree to prevent the Mount Vindhya from growing further.

At last Sage Agastya reached close to Vindhya and said: "O Great Mount! We all know your capabilities. But give me passage to visit south and stay as you are till I return."

Mount agreed to do so. But it was a trick, for Agastya never returned from south. He had gone there to spread the Great Goddess' worship. He succeeded there as much there as to drop the idea of coming back to month.

Then on being requested, Narayan told Narada the legend about the Goddess Brahmari.

Goddess Brahmari's Story

The son of Swaroclish (the Manu), Chakshusha, was installed as the Lord of the sixth Manvatar. He wanted to know the secret of prolonging his rule to almost an eternal period. The sage Pulaha advised him to worship only Super Goddess for only. "She is capable of blessing such a rile."

Following this advice he repaired to a lonely Jungle where he began to worship the Goddess with one-pointed concentration. The Goddess eventually blessed him with such a rule. By her grace the 7th Manu was Vaivaswata Manu. It was his descendants during whose reign to Goddess Bharamari had put in an appearance.

Once a demon from Petal had his good sense as much prevailing that he started chanting Gayatri Mantra and worship the Creator sitting on the bank of the river Ganga. With his 10,000 year long vigorous penance he managed to propitiate Brahma who blessed him that it would be beyond the capacity of any twin-legged being (man) or four-legged being (animals) to kill him. Getting this boon he became arrogant enough to even challenge the divine chief, Indra. Since he was not syllable either by man or beast, he created a havoc in the world. After much consultation the divine Guru Brahaspati advised that demon lord that since "by Chanting Gayatri you are as God as we divinities are. But the Gods don't accept you still. Then don't follow their path; stop chanting the Holy Mantra and devise some independent method to asset your independence." Duped by

Vrihaspati he ceased Chanting the Gayatri Mantra and became totally powerless. On the other hand, the Gods had started worshipping the Super Goddess with redoubled zeal. The Goddess, propitiated by Gods worship, adopted the form of a deadly bee (Bhramari) and hit that demon-Lord to death. Since then, Bhramari Devi came to be adored as one of the forms of the Super Goddess. Concluding the story Narayan said: "O Narad! Worship always that Goddess who cares most for his devotees."

Thus telling the legend to Raja Janmejaya, the sage Vyas told him: "If a man maintains his chosen path religious by and doesn't deviate his concentration from worshipping the Super Goddess, he attains Moksha."

Then on Janmejaya's asking Vyas Ji told him about the daily routine that a man should maintain. In the course of his narration he told the king that after bath a man should don the garland of the Rudraksha or one big head of it for escaping all kind of distractions. "Rudraksha helps in maintaining one's undivided concentration." Whereupon, Janmejaya wanted to know about this superb head, Rudraksha[1].

Origin of Rudraksha

Then the sage Vyas told him about this seeds' origin. When the demon Tripura trounced the divine Kingdom and threw out the Gods, they went straight to Lord Shiv end recited their tale of woe. Hearing it, while still in meditation, Lord Shiv happened to shed tears out of compassion. The tears from his eyes fell on the earth and in no time trees emerged having this bead. Hence they came to be known as Rudraksha. [While literally means Lord Shiv's eyes].

The sage Vyas then explained that a brahman should wear a white Rudraksha while the Kshatriyas the one with red tinge the Vaishya of mixed colours and a shoodra of dark colour, "This bead or rosery should be purified by washing first in milk, Ganga water and then five products from a cow's body (Panchagavya) while Chanting the holy Mantra "OM NAMAH SHIVAAYA"! "Wearing

---

1. The seeds of the tree Eheocarpees Ganitrees.

a Rudraksha is as efficacious as not only to keep on healthy but also fulfil the aspirants all desires," he declared.

Narrating a tale highlighting the Rudraksha's virtues sage Vyas told: "Once a mule, while carrying the weight of a sackful Rudraksha died on way, out of sheer exhaustion. When the messenger of Lord of Death came to snatch its soul away they were prevented by Lord Shiv's messenger. Eventually the mule's soul went to Shiv's realm owing to it maintaining a constant contact with the holy heads." Vyas Ji added further: "this episode was related by Lord Shiv to Skanda himself. So you can imagine how pious these beads are and how dear they are to Lord Shiv."

The same way much importance is accorded to pious Bhasm (ashes). The Purana records a narration by Narayan that once Durvasa having his entire body be semeared with Bhasm happened to pass through the Kumbheepak hell. All the mortal beings, who were being tortured there, became totally happy when a few bits of the Bhasm happened to fall from the sage's body and touch theirs. Since then by the order of Yama those with holy ash covering their body were denied admission to the hells.

Conclusion

Having told all about the ideal daily routine that a devotee of the Super Goddess should maintain, sage Vyas further emphasised the illumitable glory of the Great Goddess. "O King", he said, "Deem this whole Universe instinct with that Primal Power's presence. All births and death, creation and distractions become possible only at the implying from that Goddess. She is the Ultimate limit for all devotes no matter which deity be their chosen deity. All the Gods including Brahma, Vishnu, Mahesh act derivating their basic power from Her only."

Once drunk in the wine of arrogance and deeming them to be the ultimate source of all power through which they defeated the demons repeatedly, Brahma, Vishnu and Mahesh decided to forgo their obeisance to the Goddess. All of a sudden they found a powerful Yaksha confronting them who appeared so brilliant and powerful as to reduce all the Gods to being mere shadows. Indra then despatched the five-God to burn that Yaksha to death. The Yaksha challenged the five-God to show his strength by Burning a tiny bit of wood. Though fire God generated enough heat, he failed to even heat up that bit. When the fire-God reported his failure, the divine Chief realised that it was the Great Goddess's way of assuring Her power to teach all Gods a lesson. This made all the Gods, led by Brahma, Vishnu and Mahesh invoke Her through chanting the following Gayatri dedicated Mantra.

"Aagacchha Varade Devi Gayatri Brahmaroopini Jayaamishthan Siddhayartha, Pravish Hridayan Mam

Telling thus the glories of the Great Goddess, Soota Ji also concluded his narration by invoking collectively the Goddess and singing her Greatness. He told the assembled sages that as soon Vyas Ji concluded his enlighting discourse, he gave Janmejaya a Beej Mantra to worship the Great Goddess. Janmejaya started chanting it repeatedly. Soon he found Narad before him with the gratulatory news that Janmejaya's father, Parikshit, who was fatally bitten by the serpent Takshaka, finally left for heaven since his (Janmejaya's) listening to this Holy Devi Bhagwat Purana redeemed him from all sins. Soota Ji further emphasise that "this holy Purana is very effecacious to take care of all the mortal affictious and hence should be read and recited by the devout in their hour of distress." It should be twice read completely in a span of one year preferably at the two prominent Nawratras. So did all the sages and Chanting the Great Goddess's most enlightening Purana, all of them returned to their respective hermitages.

❑❑❑

The Puranas are the tomes that contain not only the legends to clarify the concept of true Dharma or the rightous order for clearing our cobwel of mistaken norms of life but also instruct us in leading life in an ideal way at every stage. They reveal, in an engrossing way, the gems of our ancient wisdom and as such, are ever relevant. Written in a simple language and lucid style, all-those who are willing to search their roots that formed their basic psyche would find them as an in dispessable inheritance to their 'temporarily uprooted' descendants.

Divine Gems

Message of Upanishads
Dr. B. B. Paliwal

Upanishads are the epitome of eternal knowledge. They form the treasure-trove of the sacred Vedic philosophy. Upanishads are the beacon light of all spiritual knowledge dealing with the universe and life—about creation, birth and death as well as time and space. The whole existence revolves around this eternal truth which is the metaphysical tenet of life. This knowledge is delineated in a comprehensible format in this book for the common readers. Upanishads are the gift of India to the entire world. Price : Rs. 150/-

Message of Vedas
Dr. B. B. Paliwal

In the common parlance 'Vedas' means 'knowledge'. These sacred tomes are the beacon lights of enlightenment which dispel the darkness of ignorance from the human minds. The trove of ancient Indian philosophy and culture. The mysteries of the universe, creation and existence, the time-space relationship all such metaphysical tenets are delineated in the Vedas. This book is an attempt to simplify the intriguing tenets of the Vedas into a comprehensive version for the benefit of the common readers. Price : Rs. 150/-

Message of Purans
Dr. B. B. Paliwal

In the Purans, the story of creation has been delineated in great detail. Purans are the timeless tomes of the secrets of the universe and life—about the mysterious dimensions of time and space—about the animate and the inanimate as well as about the flora and the fauna. The Purans tell you what happened in the past, what is happening in the present and what will happen in the future. Price : Rs. 150.00

: BOOKS FOR CHILDREN :

B. K. Chaturvedi
- Tales from Ramayan 95.00
- Tales from the Vedas 95.00

Mahesh Sharma
- Tales from Mahabhart 95.00
- Tales from Puranas 95.00
- Tales from the Upanishads 95.00

Books can be requisitioned by V.P.P. Postage charges will be Rs. 20/- per book. For orders of three books the postage will be free.

◉ DIAMOND POCKET BOOKS (P.) Ltd.
X-30, Okhla Industrial Area, Phase-II, Phone : 011-41611861-5, Fax : 011-41611866
E-mail : sales@diamondpublication.com, Website : www.diamondpublication.com

व्यक्तित्व विकास की श्रेष्ठ पुस्तकें

डायमंड बुक्स X-30, ओखला इंडस्ट्रियल एरिया, फेज़-II नई दिल्ली-110020 फोन : 011- 40712200
ई-मेल : sales@dpb.in   Shop online at www.diamondbook.in

डायमंड बुक्स
नवीनतम साहित्य

डायमंड बुक्स X-30, ओखला इंडस्ट्रियल एरिया, फेज-II नई दिल्ली-110020 फोन : 011-40712100
ई-मेल : sales@dpb.in   Shop online at www.diamondbook.in

www.ingramcontent.com/pod-product-compliance
Lightning Source LLC
LaVergne TN
LVHW011211080426
835508LV00007B/718